HISTORICITY AND VARIATION IN CREOLE STUDIES

Edited by
Arnold Highfield
Albert Valdman

Historicity and Variation in Creole Studies

1981

KAROMA PUBLISHERS, INC., ANN ARBOR

ISBN: 0-89720-036-5 (cloth); 0-89720-037-3 (paper)

Printed in the United States of America

CONTENTS

PREFACE

This collective volume is the second of two publications emanating from the International Conference on Theoretical Orientations in Creole Studies held in St. Thomas, U. S. Virgin Islands, March 28-April 1, 1979, under the auspices of the National Science Foundation (Grant No. BNS 78-18441) and the sponsorship of the College of the Virgin Islands and Indiana University. The Conference, which was attended by more than 150 specialists representing about twenty different nations, dealt with nine topics spanning a wide variety of theoretical and applied issues in the field of creolistics.

The St. Thomas Conference holds in the rejuvenated field of pidgin and creole studies a place comparable to that of the Mona (Jamaica) Conference of 1968. The latter, which made a wide impact on the community of linguists through the intermediary of Dell Hymes's aptly entitled compendium *Pidginization and Creolization of Languages* (London: Cambridge University Press, 1971), signaled a radical shift of direction. Up to that time the field of pidgin and creole studies had been, as its name implied, devoted to the identification and description of pidgin and creole languages. The small group of scholars who gathered at Mona oriented research away from narrow taxonomic and descriptivist concerns toward broader theoretical issues. They placed greater importance on the nature of the processes—pidginization and creolization—that produced pidgins and creoles than on the particular linguistic stages that emerged.

The seminal notions launched at Mona produced, in the following decade, a florescence of studies dealing with a much wider set of topics than those represented in the pages of *Pidginization and Creolization of Languages.* More powerful and more broadly encompassing theories were brought to bear on more delicate and more authentic pidgin and creole data. To more searching descriptions in the well-tilled fields of phonology, morphology, and lexicon were added sallies into the potentially rewarding new fields of discourse structure and pragmatics. The debate on the origins of creole languages, which for many years had pitted monogenesis against polygenesis, was enriched by the injection of new currents, for example: the neurobiological, characterized by appeal to linguistic universals, to general principles of first- and second-language acquisition; the sociohistorical, marked by careful documentation of the settlement history of the plantation colonies and the reconstruction of the social matrix in which creoles developed. The emergence of new creole-speaking nations (e.g., Mauritius, Papua-New Guinea, the Seychelles) and a rising tide of nationalism in other creolophone territories, still dominated culturally, economically, or politically by European metropoles or the United States, have brought to the fore the question of the use of the local creole or pidgin in domains (education, mass media, administrative services) that had been held exclusively by a dominant West European language (often the creole's or the pidgin's lexical-base language).

Many of these newer issues and topics were treated at international gatherings, some of which led to the publication of collective volumes: Georgetown University, 1971 (D. DeCamp and I. F. Hancock, eds., *Pidgins and Creoles: Current Trends and Prospects,* Washington, DC: Georgetown University Press, 1973); the International Conference on Pidgins and Creoles (Honolulu, 1975); the First Symposium of the Society for Caribbean Linguistics (G. Cave, ed., *New Directions in Creole Studies,* Georgetown, Guyana: University of Guyana, 1976); Premier Colloque International des Etudes Créoles, Nice, 1976 (the proceedings of this colloquium, organized by the newly founded francophone Comité International des Etudes Créoles, appeared in the Comité's journal, *Etudes créoles*); University of Wuppertal (J. M. Meisel, ed., *Languages in Contact–Pidgins, Creoles–Langues en contact,* Tübingen: Gunter Narr, 1976). But these various gatherings tended to be regional in nature, and they did not address the full range of concerns recognized by the evolving field of creolistics.

It was to provide a truly international forum for the discussion of these new issues and topics that the International Conference on Theoretical Orientations in Creole Studies was convened in St. Thomas. The Conference was organized around nine themes falling into four groups. The first group (structural and lexical development) focused on the internal mechanisms that guide the development of creolized speech varieties. In the case of phonological and morphosyntactic complexification considerable attention was devoted to the relationship between simplification and markedness. That choice of perspective reflected the growing acceptance on the part of specialists of the fact that in accounting for the genesis and development of creole languages the delineation of grammatical complexification and lexical expansion will prove to be more central than the issue of monogenesis versus polygenesis. That approach also forces one to deal squarely with the question of whether internal developmental processes observable in creolization are different in nature or scope from those that operate in the evolution of "normal," natural languages. The discussion of these two topics led to the useful opposition of early-creolizing languages, such as the Caribbean creoles, to late-creolizing languages (also termed elaborated pidgins), such as Tok Pisin. That distinction promises to introduce greater clarity in assessing the contribution of linguistic universals and general processes of language acquisition to the genesis of creoles, for these are more applicable to early- rather than late-creolizing varieties. Related to the first group of themes were the topics "Creolization and Linguistic Change" and "Creolization and Second-Language Acquisition." The popularity enjoyed currently by creole studies stems in large part from the promise they hold for shedding new light on linguistic change and for clarifying the distinction between first- and second-language acquisition. The inclusion of the latter topic marked the link between creolistics and the field of second-language acquisition and learning effected by applied linguists who have espoused the view that those basic principles which determined the course of first-language acquisition still operate, at least to a certain degree, in adult second-language learning. A strong impetus for that junction was provided by research on Gastarbeiter Deutsch undertaken by several teams in West Germany, two of which (Heidelberg and Wuppertal/Hamburg) were represented in St. Thomas in the persons of N. Dittmar and J. M. Meisel, respectively. A revised version of their interventions appears in *Studies in Second Language Acquisition* 3(2), which features Gastarbeiter Deutsch studies.

The third group of themes centered on the problem of variation in creolized speech varieties: the creole continuum, decreolization, and sociolinguistic orientations. The sociolinguistic perspective dominating this group reflected the downgrading of the traditional notion of the creole life-cycle according to which the principal parameter of variation in creole studies is that which demarcates structural stages: pre-pidgin, pidgin, pre-creole, creole, and post-creole. It also underscored the need to sort out the respective influence of external factors (social forces and language contact) and internal mechanisms (linguistic universals and processes of internal development) in triggering creolization and in the crystallization of discrete linguistic objects.

The last group of themes (language planning and educational issues) was included in response to new political forces manifesting themselves in creolophone communities. The use of a creole or an expanded pidgin in domains previously reserved for dominant West European languages poses problems of standardization (codification and reduction of variation) and instrumentalization (development of orthographies, lexical enrichment, and stylistic diversification). In the educational sphere it also necessitates choices among alternative bilingual models which, while recognizing differences in political power, social prestige, and degree of instrumentalization between the creole or expanded pidgin and the established, "normal" language(s) of the community, make room for the former. In underdeveloped countries, such as Haiti, where the preponderant majority of the population consists of monolingual speakers of the creole, the choice of the appropriate bilingual model results in more rapid and effective literacy without denying to monolingual speakers of creole access to the dominant language. The extended use of the creole also satisfies strong political pressures arising from newly gained statehood or increased participation in national affairs that endow the creole with symbolic value.

In this connection the St. Thomas Conference marked a radical departure from preceding international gatherings of creolists. Although the fact is not clearly reflected in this volume (note, however, that of the twenty-one contributions to *Theoretical Orientations in Creole Studies* six were prepared by "native" creolists, compared to seven out of thirty-eight in *Pidginization and Creolization of Languages* published a decade earlier), native speakers of creole languages outnumbered foreign linguists. The relatively low proportion of the former had become a serious concern in a field whose objects of study, situated in Third World countries, are associated with economic underdevelopment and political dependence. Perhaps the most noteworthy aspect of the St. Thomas Conference was the participation of a dozen professionals in language planning and education from Haiti. In the course of impassioned contributions to the discussion in the sessions on these two topics, they did not hesitate, in a predominantly anglophone scientific gathering, to resort to their vernacular tongue, thus providing dramatic demonstration of the adequacy and suitability of Haitian Creole for scholarly discourse. In the "native" versus "foreign" linguist issue in the field of creolistics it is not that native control of a creole automatically renders the analysts' descriptive observations more authoritative or their theoretical pronouncements more insightful; rather membership in a creolophone community makes them more sensitive to the economic, social, and, especially, political implications of language choice and of language variation. It also leads them to adopt theoretical models and methodological procedures that do not arbitrarily separate linguistic facts and sociolinguistic data from the functioning of the creole in the community and its role in the demarcation of social groups.

Each of the St. Thomas Conference's nine main sessions was organized around a position paper circulated to participants in advance. The discussion of each theme comprised a discussant report and a small number of short interventions, distributed in full form and presented at the Conference in summary version, treating a restricted aspect of the central theme. The seven contributions assembled in this volume address the first three groups of topics of the Conference. They deal with the nature of the linguistic continuum between creolized varieties and co-existent lexical-base languages, the relative contribution of internal factors and external contact, differences between creolization and normal linguistic change, and the relationship between creolization and social identity. They focus on several types of variation found in creole languages, and they attempt to sort out the relative import of the lexical-base language, the substrate languages, and general evolutive processes in the formation of creoles. Finally, they provide a representative view of narrowly focused work, undertaken mostly by younger workers, which addresses the central issues in creolistics. Thus, together they serve to complement the more encompassing position papers and discussant reports appearing in *Theoretical Orientations in Creole Studies* (A. Valdman and A. R. Highfield, eds., New York: Academic Press, 1980). These seven contributions were selected from among the more than forty presented at and/or circulated in advance of the Conference on the basis of their compatibility with the theme of this volume, *Historicity and Variation in Creole Studies,* and of the rankings given by an international committee charged with the screening of interventions submitted to the Conference.

Elizabeth C. Traugott, whose organization of an international conference on historical linguistics prevented her from attending the St. Thomas gathering, was the obvious choice for introducing this volume. The author of several distinguished articles on the relationship between creolization and language change, she has also been boldly innovative in relating linguistic structure to broader aspects of verbal communication. We would like to thank her for agreeing to comment on the papers from the perspective of the study of linguistic change and the development of creole studies.

The organization of the St. Thomas Conference would not have been possible without the generous support of the NSF and our institutions, the College of the Virgin Islands and Indiana University. We would also like to acknowledge a debt of gratitude to the many colleagues at the St. Croix and St. Thomas campuses of the College of the Virgin Islands and to friends from the "autochthonous" linguistic communities of St. Thomas who cheerfully provided assistance and support.

Arnold Highfield
Albert Valdman
June 1981

INTRODUCTION

Elizabeth Closs Traugott
Stanford University

Since the publication in Hymes (1971) of the proceedings of the 1968 Mona Conference on Pidginization and Creolization of Languages, pidgin and creole studies have emerged as important challenges to linguistic theory and method. By definition pidgins and creoles involve language mix; therefore, they challenge the assumption of homogeneity espoused by most mainstream linguistic theory, in the United States at least, since de Saussure. Because they develop rapidly, these, and other varieties of language mix, are ideal environments in which to study variation, not only synchronically but also through time. Whereas phonetic change in progress is relatively easy to observe among traditionally studied languages, morphological, syntactic, and especially pragmatic changes such as the development of discourse styles and discourse markers are relatively hard to observe. In many pidgins and creoles, however, observable changes in these areas are the norm rather than the exception. Pidgins and creoles are therefore of vital importance to historical studies, while at the same time they raise both theoretical questions concerning appropriate models for change and methodological questions concerning the validity of projecting observed changes in progress back on the past. The papers in this volume address several of the issues concerning variation through both space ("synchronic variation") and time ("diachronic variation"). Like other studies of language variation in the last decade (and indeed since de Saussure first formalized the dichotomy between synchrony and diachrony), they suggest that the study of synchrony, an admittedly hypothetical steady state, can and must be informed by the study of change, and that ultimately only a dynamic model will explain the nature of language (cf. Bailey 1973).

A study of processes of pidginization, creolization, and decreolization highlights for the researcher the importance of continua in linguistic structure (cf. DeCamp 1971, Bickerton 1975). But continua are by no means restricted to linguistic structure. Despite many attempts to define the terms "pidgin" and "creole" in homogeneous ways, they have proved to defy such definition; our metalanguage too must admit of continua. Whereas some linguists would term any mixture "creolization" (e.g., Bailey and Maroldt 1977), others would prefer to differentiate very precisely the various types of language process arising out of various types of contact. Whinnom (1971), for example, restricts pidginization and subsequent creolization to many-to-one contact occurring under circumstances of minimal social integration between the speakers of the many (substrate) languages and the one (superstrate) language. In this volume, "creole studies" is used in a fairly broad sense, covering languages developing not only from many-to-one situations (e.g., Dominican Creole, Pidgin Swahili), but also from one-to-one situations (e.g., Media Lengua, a contact language arising from a mixture of Quechua and Spanish), provided only that social inequality is present.

Several papers focus on how one type of language mix changes into another. Whether or not a stable pidgin arises is shown to be a function of whether a pidgin target arises (Wald). Such a target, Wald suggests, comes into being only when a first language vernacular target is absent, that is, when there is no first language which functions as the prestige norm. This distinction is useful when explaining why some languages, e.g., Hawaiian Pidgin, stabilized very little (English was the indisputable target vernacular), while others like Tok Pisin and Pidgin Swahili did stabilize. In the case of Tok Pisin, no single New Guinea language was an indisputable vernacular target. Similarly, in Coastal Kenya, neither vernacular Swahili nor Standard Swahili is considered a target since the former is identified with relatively small ethnic groups and the latter is largely inaccessible, being the product of formal education. Wald further suggests that stabilized pidgins may undergo depidginization as speakers shift to another, vernacular target. This shift may involve extensive elaboration, but not creolization.

What then *is* creolization? While often identified with nativization of a language that is more elaborate grammatically and stylistically than a pidgin, but different from any target first language vernacular in the area (cf. Bickerton 1975, Mühl-haüsler 1980), it has also been identified with mere elaboration of a pidgin without nativization (e.g., Sankoff and Brown 1976). The difference between depidginization without creolization, on the one hand, and a shift from pidgin status to creole status, on the other, can be directly explained in terms of the target. In the first case it is a vernacular target; in the second, it is not. Baudet reminds us that yet another possibility for creolization in many-to-one language mix is abrupt creolization without an intermediary pidgin stage. Support for such a hypothesis comes, she argues, from the extensive typological similarity of certain creoles, in this case those of the Caribbean, with phonological, morphological, and syntactic characteristics of West African languages, a similarity too great to justify the assumption of an intermediate pidgin different in structure from such languages. How such typologies came to be crystallized into any one language system, however, must continue to be a matter of debate, and one that will have to take into consideration the growing evidence for West African pidgins with a variety of target lexicons (cf. Hancock 1969).

While the question of definition and characterization of certain language types is an important issue in many of the papers in this volume, several other questions recur. They may be grouped under the following headings: causes of change, mechanisms of change, types of change, and incorporation of evidence for language change into a sociohistorical theory of language (cf. the "actuation," "transition," "constraints," and "embedding" problems identified in Weinreich, Labov and Herzog 1968).

The causes and mechanisms of pidginization and creolization have been the focus of much attention from the beginning of creole studies. The most commonly cited cause of pidginization is language mix resulting from communicative needs in situations of either social asymmetry or mutual unintelligibility (for a focus on inter-group communication, see Cassidy 1971 and Manessy, this volume). Muysken, however, suggests that inter-group communication may be only a partial cause of pidginization in many situations. Inter-group communicative needs would lead, he argues, to massive adoption of target language structures. Words would be borrowed not only with the phonological characteristics of the target language, but also with its semantic and syntactic structure (a process which he calls "translexification"). A close look at some pidgins shows, however, the continued presence of substrate syntax and semantics; lexical items frequently have the surface phonetic form of the target language, but not the semantic or syntactic features typical of this target language (this process he calls "relexification"). These facts suggest that intra-group communication may be as important in the process of pidginization as inter-group communication, at least in some cases. Native structures are maintained, in other words, for cultural identity. The data Muysken uses from Media Lengua illustrate language mix of the one-to-one type, so it remains to be seen whether the analysis can be projected onto many-to-one types of language mix as in the case of the Caribbean languages; but if it can, it may suggest why the typological characteristics of African languages that Baudet sees in Caribbean creoles may have been retained even if there was an intermediary pidgin stage (cf. LePage 1977 on the importance of "intra-actions" leading to cultural focusing, at the creole stage).

Muysken challenges traditional views of not only the causes of pidginization but also the mechanism of pidginization. This mechanism is usually thought to be a process of second language acquisition accompanied by considerable interference from the native language (cf. Bickerton 1977; also Schumann 1978, Andersen forthcoming). Muysken argues that since acquisition of L_2 has a fairly high degree of similarity with processes of L_1 acquisition, and interference from the native language is usually fairly low (Hatch 1978), it is difficult to understand how so much native language structure is to be found in pidgins and creoles. What is usually termed interference in creole studies is, Muysken claims, actually translexification (that is, retention for expressive purposes). Further research on differences between structured second language acquisition in the classroom and "natural" second language acquisition in unstructured situations may reveal, however, that low degrees of interference are a function of natural acquisition, and that there is therefore no fundamental difficulty with the traditional view of the mechanism of pidginization.

Both Muysken and Baudet provide more evidence in support of the claim that pidgins and creoles are to be regarded as evolving out of substrate languages in contact with superstrate languages (cf. Whinnom 1971), rather than out of superstrate languages modified ("simplified") for purposes of communication with substrate speakers (cf. Hall 1966). This does not of course deny the possibility of two-way interaction (Manessy), but points to a focus of attention.

Finally, regarding mechanisms of change, it should be noted that in this volume there is virtually no discussion of questions concerning universals (cf. Bickerton 1974, Traugott 1976, Givón 1979 and, from a different point of view, Kay and Sankoff 1974). Indeed, with the exception of Baudet's paper on the typological approach to mechanisms of change, there is very little consideration of "internal" mechanisms of change, that is, mechanisms dependent primarily on linguistic neurological processes. However, differences between perception and production in language acquisition as explanations of processes of creolization are a major theme in Mühlhäusler's paper in the companion volume to this book (Mühlhäusler 1980).

Types of change and stages in their development are of concern in virtually all the papers in this volume. There is discussion of change within every subsystem of language: phonology (Escure), morphosyntax (Baudet, Escure, Morgan, Wald), lexical semantics (Holm), and the pragmatics of communicative and expressive language function (Manessy, Muysken).

One recurrent theme is the disparity in both rate and type of change between phonology and morphosyntax. Wald, for example, shows that depidginization of Pidgin Swahili involves adaptation of the morphology and syntax into a vernacular norm, but not of the phonology. Similarly, Escure shows that decreolization in Belize shows a high rate of morphosyntactic change, but a low rate of phonological change. Indeed, she suggests that creole phonological features in Belize are barely stigmatized and are in fact coming to be accepted as the norm. The independence of phonological and morphosyntactic change has long been known in historical linguistics and has been noted for language change in progress (Labov 1972a). The papers in this volume give fresh insight, however, into the way in which phonology can be less subject to prestige pressures than other parts of the linguistic system. Whether this is primarily a function of prestige forms with written norms, as Escure suggests, remains to be seen.

Another recurrent theme is the nature of lexical change. A topic often discussed in connection with pidgin and creole studies is the size and nature of the lexicon.

These are in part a function of internal changes within a system (for example, shifts in the process of word formation from compounding to derivation) and in part a function of borrowing from external sources of more and more distinct lexical items. Both cases involve expansion of semantic specificity on the one hand and of stylistic options on the other (cf. Mühlhäusler 1980). In this volume, the focus is on external factors (borrowing, relexification, translexification), and their effect on the system of the creole. Muysken focuses on the syntactic changes resulting from the borrowing of vocabulary when this is a case of translexification.

Any change can be expected to have social correlates. Ideally, these social correlates should be shown to be of the causal type. In other words, a language changes in response to social changes in the lives and aspirations of its speakers. Alone, it does not create new social situations. Therefore, one would like to be able to show what social situations can give rise to what changes (cf. Sankoff 1980; Trudgill in preparation). However, any such explanation is problematic at the microlevel of particular changes. As was mentioned above, on the macro-level, social intermixing or problems of social identity are shown in this volume to have a causal relation in the process of pidginization and creolization (Muysken, Wald); so are communicative and expressive needs, given certain contexts (Escure, Manessy, Muysken).

One of the reasons that the exact role of social factors in any particular case of language change is difficult to assess is that current sociolinguistic theory has not yet fully integrated the study of nonlinguistic contexts such as age, sex, and social stratification (cf. Labov 1972a) with the study of discourse contexts (cf. Gumperz 1977). Most importantly, while Labov has stressed the importance of projecting the present back onto the past (1974), serious sociohistorical linguistics is still in its infancy (see, however, Romaine 1980). Questions that pidgin and creole studies have started to answer (cf. Chaudenson 1977) include:

1. Are social situations comparable across cultures and ages? Are the situations that gave rise to pidgins and creoles in Hawaii or New Guinea in any way comparable with each other, or with those of foreign workers in contemporary Europe? Are any of these comparable to the slave situation that gave rise to pidgins and creoles in the Caribbean?

2. How does one project back onto the past when detailed information about social stratification, education, sex roles, and so forth is largely lacking, and when there is virtually no information about social networks? Does historical linguistics have to focus on a stylistic continuum without adequate reference to social parameters? (And what, indeed, is "style"?)

3. How can we reconcile changes that occurred primarily in the spoken medium with data that are available to us only in the written medium? In the one paper in

this volume which directly addresses the question of reconstructing the precise interrelationships between the development of a language and its social history, Holm focuses on one aspect of the latter question—how to use a dictionary such as the *Oxford English Dictionary* (based on written materials) and the *English Dialect Dictionary* (based on spoken materials) to determine the period at which and regions from which lexical items were borrowed into Nicaragua's Miskito Coast Creole.

Changing as rapidly as they do, the languages which are the subject of creole studies promise not only to provide much valuable evidence for how language changes in contemporary societies, but also to suggest ways of implementing and constraining the projection of current change in progress onto the past.

SWAHILI PRE-PIDGIN, PIDGIN, AND DEPIDGINIZATION IN COASTAL KENYA
A Systematic Discontinuity in Non-First Varieties of Swahili

Benji Wald
University of California, Los Angeles

1. Introduction. The primary purpose of this article is to compare first and non-first varieties of Swahili spoken in Coastal Kenya, in order to show that for the particular grammatical features to be considered, there are two distinct grammatical systems used by speakers, one of which will be identified as Pidgin Swahili (PS) and the other as First Swahili (FS). When linguistically mature new learners acquire Swahili, their target is PS. Under the influence of FS speakers and prior depidginizing speakers, coastal PS speakers assimilate FS linguistic norms, thus changing their target variety of Swahili. All Swahili speakers, including FS speakers, take advantage of the PS bridge for communication. As a multilingual phenomenon, the coastal situation of the interaction of PS and FS presents a hitherto undescribed case of an intermediate language (PS) mitigating the acquisition of a vernacular target language.

1.1. Language acquisition in multilingual situations. Generally, investigators have tacitly assumed that multilingual situations are of two invariant types with respect to language acquisition. They are discussed here under the headings of (1) vernacular target and (2) pidgin target.

1. *Vernacular target.* A new group of a different language background aims at the first language target of the host community. The early stages of acquisition may resemble pidgin versions of the host language, and some new learners may arrest acquisition at such a stage, giving rise to the notion that pidgins may, perhaps must, originate in this way. This approach is most pronounced among students of second language acquisition. For example, concerning the acquisition of English in the United States, particularly among Spanish speakers, it is noted that the early characteristics of such English, e.g., lack of inflections and the distinct means of negation, resemble those of English pidgins spoken elsewhere, e.g., West Africa, the Pacific area. However, it is assumed that these speakers are not exposed to any stable English pidgin, but rather that they naturally go through these stages in pursuing a First English target (cf. Schumann 1978). The work of the Heidelberger Project (1978) on the speech of foreign workers acquiring German, the case of an *industrial* pidgin, does not directly confront this issue but orders speakers

by degree of sentence complexity approaching the first language target. The question of the target's being a previously established German pidgin is not discussed, but it is implicit that no such pidgin is suspected, although it may at this point in time be developing. The theory that the vernacular target is the origin of a pidgin was effectively posed by Whinnom (1971) in the contrast between *cocoliche,* a stereotype of the Spanish of new learners of Italian background in Buenos Aires, and stable pidgins with their own independent norms of use. According to this theory, a true pidgin develops when the first language target is inaccessible, i.e., when first language speakers are withdrawn in favor of non-first speakers.

2. *Pidgin target.* In the multilingual situation associated with areas of great linguistic diversity, no first language has an advantage which would lead other speakers to aim at a vernacular target. Instead there exists a pidgin which is primarily learned from other pidgin speakers. The degree to which such a pidgin may stabilize and develop a uniform set of norms across speakers became an issue of concern and of some controversy among investigators in the 1970s. The two most extensive empirical studies of this period came to different conclusions based on different local situations. In the case of New Guinea (cf. Mühlhäusler 1980, Sankoff 1980), Neo-Melanesian, an English-based pidgin, has been spoken for a considerable period of time. With increasing urbanization and its effect on surrounding rural areas, the pidgin has spread to increasing numbers of speakers of a large variety of languages. In the meantime it has innovated elaborations of its grammar among pidgin speakers independent of the language background of the speakers. It is shown that although the pidgin is now creolizing into a new first language, Tok Pisin, many of the innovations are developments within the pidgin itself rather than due to a creole restructuring. In the case of Hawaiian Pidgin English, especially for Japanese and Filipino immigrants, no stable pidgin grammar has evolved (Bickerton and Odo 1976-77). The authors emphasize that many grammatical structures show variation which can best be explained as importations from the first languages of the speakers. Although elements common to Pacific English-based pidgins (including Neo-Melanesian) are identifiable, e.g., the use of *stei* and *stap* as locative and aspect markers, uniformity of use and stability occur only for the creole generation. It is proposed that in some cases pidgin speakers have assimilated creole targets but that there is no clear pidgin target grammar. The presence of First English in the environment affects both pidgin and creole speakers so that no uniform pidgin target has had time to develop.

1.2. Pidgin Swahili in Mombasa. PS is spoken throughout Kenya. In Interior Kenya a relatively uniform pidgin is spoken in the absence of any sizable community of FS speakers. The target of new speakers is the pidgin.

A virtually identical Swahili pidgin is also spoken in Coastal Kenya, particularly in the port city of Mombasa, to which the major research presented here is localized. Mombasa is the site of an FS speech community of long and continuous tradition.

Of the approximately 250,000 people living in Mombasa in the mid-1970s, only about 38 percent are native to the city. We estimate that no more than 15 percent of the total population are FS speakers.[1] There is no ethnic majority in Mombasa, where first language is closely linked to ethnicity. The Bantu-speaking Miji Kenda, 24 percent of the population, originating in the rural areas around Mombasa and in intimate contact with FS speakers for several centuries, are generally colingual in the ethnic language and a form of Swahili very similar to FS. They constitute the largest ethnic-like unit in the city and are not PS speakers.

We estimate that PS is spoken by about 60 percent of the population. Among its speakers, the Interior Kenyan groups of Bantu and Nilotic background (collectively 33 percent of the population) form the majority of PS speakers. Indo-European speakers, principally Gujerati-speaking Asians forming 16 percent of the population, are largely PS speakers. Semitic and Kushitic speakers of Southern Arabian, Somalian, and Ethiopian language background, collectively constitute 6 percent of the population. About half this group speaks PS rather than FS.

There is little direct motivation for non-FS speakers to aim at an FS target. FS is an ethnic language distinct from both PS, the universal Kenyan lingua franca, and Standard Swahili, a product of formal education in Kenya. Command of FS norms is highly valued among FS ethnic groups but not among immigrants. It is not a vehicle of opportunity for most, since most economic activity takes place among non-FS speakers and most FS speakers do not occupy visible or desirable positions in the economic structure of the city.

Immigrants tend to settle in areas where coethnic communities have already taken root, giving them opportunity to continue communication in their first languages. Nevertheless, FS speakers are found everywhere, although in varying degrees of density according to neighborhood, and their cultural and linguistic presence is felt by all inhabitants. Although many coethnics and other non-FS speakers inevitably found in immigrant neighborhoods continue to use PS norms in their speech, increasing elaboration of the pidgin grammar indicates a process of depidginization toward an FS target.

The importance of Swahili in Mombasa is expressed by PS speakers in commonly used phrases such as "in Mombasa you hafta know Swahili," and "everybody knows Swahili in Mombasa." This does not specify what *kind* of Swahili, but it distinguishes the coastal situation in the minds of migrants from the interior, where competition between Swahili and English is more intense on the overt level of job opportunities. PS speakers overwhelmingly judge their own Swahili as "bad" (*mbovu* 'rotten'; FS speakers generally agree that PS speakers *haribu* 'ruin' Swahili), but vary in their concern toward this "defect." Most likely the judgment is an adoption of FS attitudes which are quick to distinguish FS, associated with the coast *(pwani)*, from the pidginized varieties of Swahili associated with *Bara* 'Interior Kenya'. In accepting FS judgments, PS speakers overtly identify PS as a "bad" variety of Swahili, typical of societies where a pidgin and its base are both present. However, because of the ethnic symbolism of FS, most speakers are covertly unconcerned with their use of Swahili and find PS adequate for their purposes. I found that many PS speakers were aware upon reflection of many of the FS norms, such as class concord, but they rarely or never used them in their own speech.[2] Thus, PS is currently more secure in Mombasa than overt evaluation of its speakers might lead one to believe.

2. **Criteria for Pidgin Swahili.** PS is defined in this study by both social and linguistic criteria. Speakers of PS were identified by:

a. *Time of acquisition.* The speaker is not an FS speaker. For the moment, Foreigner Talk, the style or register of Swahili used by FS speakers to address new learners, is excluded from PS, although it will be shown that it shares features with PS not found in other styles of FS (cf. Ferguson and DeBose 1977).

b. *Context of acquisition.* The speaker acquired Swahili in a nonscholastic context, i.e., not by the planned and reasoned instruction of formal education.[3]

Under these nonlinguistic conditions, we find a variety of Swahili, PS, which agrees with the system for Kenyan Interior Pidgin Swahili abstracted by Heine (1973) from the speech of Interior PS speakers. Its most salient grammatical characteristics are:

a. Obligatory grammatical categories of FS are either totally or variably absent in PS, e.g., the subject marker (SM), the object marker (OM).

b. A tense marker (TM) is obligatory in PS but reduced to a single marker, *na* (phonetically [na]), in contrast to no marking of the verb at all. FS has an elaborate paradigm of TMs.

c-1. A lack of obligatory syntactic processes, e.g., PS uses ∅ or *ile* (a stereotyped form of the obviate demonstrative 'that') for marking relativization rather than the complex FS pattern.

c-2. The use of stereotyped, unanalyzed markers rather than a system of concordial markers sensitive to the class of the controlling noun phrase, characteristic of FS as of Bantu languages in general.

The following example contrasts a sentence spoken by a paradigmatic PS speaker with its FS equivalent, illustrating several differences between the two systems:

/1a/ *PS Sentence:*
saa–ile–[mbwa–na-kufa]–ye–na-ona–na-sema–na–kweli–hii–mama-ngu–na-kufa
time–that–[dog–TM-die]–he–TM-see–TM-say–Cop–true–this–mother-my–TM-die
"When he saw the dead dog, he said, 'It's true that my mother has died.' "
(Z:26f, Somali)[4]

/1b/ *FS Equivalent:*
(ye)–a-li-po-(mw-)–ona–[(yule)–mbwa–a-me-kufa]–a-ka-sema–ni–kweli–(kwamba)–mama-ngu–a-me-kufa
(he)–SM-Past-when-(OM-)–see–(the)–dog–SM-Perf-die–SM-then-say–Cop–true–compl–mother-my–SM-Perf-die

We first note from examples /1a/ and /1b/ that PS preserves some of the inflection of FS. Thus, there is a TM, indeed the unique TM *na,* prefixed to the verb, and there is a paradigm of personal possessives suffixed to the possessed noun; these suffixed possessives are distinct in form from the independent pronoun paradigm of PS. These features are found in all varieties of PS, coastal or interior, and are perhaps surprising in contrast to the greater reduction of inflection of European-based pidgins.[5]

In focusing attention on the differences between FS and PS to be pursued in this paper, we now turn to the SM and the TM. In PS, the most frequent, and for many the only, TM is *na,* as in /1a/ above. This contrasts with no (∅) TM marking for a negative or imperative verb, and, for most speakers, also with the infinitive verbal prefix *ku-*. It is used in all cases where FS would use one of a number of TMs, of which three distinct TMs are featured in example /1b/: *li* 'past' (actually 'anterior' in FS); *me* 'perfective'; and *ka* 'consecutive'. The occurrence of an obligatory TM is quite interesting in PS since in FS it conditions an obligatory SM which must be immediately prefixed to it as in /1b/. However, in PS, as seen in /1a/, there is no category of SM whereby the TM is not preceded by any inflection. Anticipating later discussion of depidginization, the existence of the TM in PS provides the structure to which SM marking is prefixed when it is acquired.

3. On the stability and uniformity of PS. All the features of PS discussed above are uniform regardless of the area in which PS is spoken. Features such as the TM and possessive suffixes are specific and cannot be ascribed to independent pidgin developments in different areas. This establishes a specific PS target for new learners of Swahili. Speakers must be exposed to PS norms in order to learn them. Given the social habits of new learners as discussed in section **1.2** above, their first target is the PS of coethnics and cohabitants.

3.1. The pre-pidgin stage. An example of a new learner of Swahili is AY:22m,

Somali. He arrived in Mombasa during the period of my research without prior exposure to Swahili. After a month on the streets, he exhibited few features that characterize stable PS. His language resembled the early stages in the acquisition of German by foreign workers, in which verbless utterances predominate over verbful ones (Heidelberger 1978). Given that his target is the PS of his associates in Mombasa, he may be said to speak *pre-pidgin.* SMs are totally absent from his speech, as indeed they are in PS. All observed verbs occurred in an invariant form. In one recorded session during a card game, 13 different verbs were used a total of 35 times. Where TM marking would be the norm in PS, AY used uninflected verbs in utterances such as:

/2a/ *Pre-Pidgin Utterance:*
karata–chese–nne
cards–play–four
"It's a *card* game that *four* people *play.*" (AY:22m, Somali)

/2b/ *Closest PS Equivalent:*
karata–hii–*na*-cheza–nne
cards–this–*TM*-play–four
"Four (people) play this card game."

The closest PS equivalent in /2b/ emphasizes that in PS the TM *na* would mark the verb.

However, two verbs occurred invariably with *na* prefixed: *na(-)jua* 'know' (8 times) and *na(-)taka* 'want' (3 times). There is no evidence that AY analyzes *na* as an independent morpheme for these verbs. As quasi-statives these two verbs are not likely to be found in uninflected form in either PS or FS, i.e., they are not likely to be used imperatively. AY's behavior suggests that TM acquisition begins with these verbs but that they are unanalyzed at first. That the TM "form" acquired is *na* indicates the pidgin source.

3.2. The evolution of PS. Little is known about the ultimate origin of PS. It is certain that the basic PS norms spread across Tanzania from a Zanzibari FS base into Eastern Zaire in the mid-19th century as part of a Swahili trade lingua franca. Many of these PS norms are preserved in the creolized Swahili, kiNgwana, spoken in Eastern Zaire. The route by which PS arrived in Interior Kenya in the early 20th century is not certain, but it is most likely that it came through Tanzania rather than directly from the Kenyan coast. One linguistic piece of evidence for this assumption is the use of the generalized TM *na* in PS. *Na* has been in the last two centuries of much more frequent usage in Tanzanian (Southern) FS than in Kenyan FS (cf. Wald 1973, 1976). Its adoption into PS as the stereotyped TM thus points to diffusion from Tanzania rather than Coastal Kenya. In Interior

Kenya the rise of PS is associated with urbanization, especially in the Nairobi area, and with a linguistically heterogeneous population (cf. Whiteley 1969). This variety of PS has greatly increased on the coast, particularly in urban Mombasa, due to the migration of PS speakers from the interior.

A slightly different variety of PS, called Northern PS here, possibly predates the use of general PS in Coastal Kenya. It is largely restricted to Northern coastal peoples, e.g., Southern Arabians and Somalis, but its distinguishing features cannot be attributed to first language influence; thus, it indicates the establishment of a localized set of pidgin norms. The few differences between general PS and Northern PS are arresting, although they are simply matters of the lexical form of grammatical morphemes. Two examples illustrate:

a. In Northern PS the form of the "unmarked" TM is *ma,* equivalent to the invariant *na* of general PS. The following speaker uses *ma* and *na* indifferently in a story he repeated twice:

/3/ basi–*ma*-rudi–*ma*-sema–mimi–ha-ku-vika–kwa–mzee
so–*TM*-return–*TM*-say–me–neg-past-arrive–at–old-man
"So he went back and said, 'I didn't get to the old man.' "

(H:43m, Arabic)

/4/ *na*-sema–*na*-ona–yule–tu–uko-uko
TM-say–*TM*-see–that–just–over-there
"She said, 'Do(n't) you see him right over there?' "

(H:43m, Arabic)

b. The form of the copula is invariant *iko* in general PS. In Northern PS *yuko* is also used as an equivalent:[6]

/5/ lugha–ya–Hadhramut–*yuko*–Qur^{c}an–ndani–ya-ke
language–of–H–*Cop*–Quran–inside–of-it
"Hadhramut (Arabic) has Quranic words in it."

(H:43m, Arabic)

The general PS copula is illustrated in /6/:

/6/ kama–dolfin–lakini–*iko*–mombamba–sana
like–dolphin–but–*Cop*–thin–very
"(It's) like a dolphin, but it's very slender."

(G:38m, Gujerati)

The dialectal variation in PS has been attended to because Northern PS has not been described before,[7] and, more to the point, it demonstrates the stability of the establishment of a PS target in East Africa. All PS speakers share the general PS norms. The Northern PS norms do not *elaborate* the grammatical system of PS although the additional variation may be viewed as a *complication* to the description of PS grammars for some speakers.

4. Elaboration of the TM system in depidginization. In this and the following sections we will observe the pattern of adoption of FS norms by several speakers of PS. In addition, we will compare the resulting elaboration, or depidginization, of PS with various styles of FS speech in Mombasa. For these purposes, four PS speakers and two FS speakers have been chosen as a data sample. Unless otherwise indicated, analyzed data will be restricted to taperecorded speech in the contexts presented in Table 1 on p. 15.[8]

Table 1 displays the number of distinct TMs used by the speakers in all observed discourse, presenting a measure of elaboration of the PS paradigm of one TM (*na*, with *ma* as a nondistinctive variant used only by H).

The PS speakers show varying degrees of elaboration of the TM system, ranging from a minimum of 2 for Z to a maximum of 5 for H. FS speech shows a drastic reduction of TMs used in Foreigner Talk (4) from the in-talk system high of 8.

To a large extent the increasing elaboration of the TM paradigm follows a distinct ordering from depidginization through the different styles of FS speech. The basic ordering is shown in Figure 1, p. 16.

The general pattern of elaboration of the TM system in PS is to add consecutively *ta, li, me,* and finally, *ki.* B presents an unusual case in that her fourth TM is *n* rather than *me.* As discussed below, *n* is the Mombasa FS vernacular equivalent of *me* found in FS out-talk. B reveals more intimate contact with the FS vernacular than do the other PS speakers. H, as noted above, also uses *ma.* Since his *ma* and *na* are equivalent pidgin norms, they count together as a single TM in terms of the number of *distinct* TMs in his system, qualifying him for no more than a 5-TM system.

MJ's pattern of Foreigner Talk shows the same degree and type of elaboration as do the depidginizing PS speakers. From the perspective of J's fluent styles of FS, Foreigner Talk shows a sharp reduction of the TM system. Less dramatic, but still striking in its categoriality, is the addition of *n* only in in-talk. As shown in detail by Wald (1973), *n* is the vernacular equivalent of *me* with which it varies in in-talk, but it is totally suppressed by most speakers in out-talk.

Despite varying degrees of elaboration in their TM systems, all PS speakers use *na,* the primary TM in PS, as the dominant TM. This is true also of FS speakers in nonvernacular styles. Table 2 on p. 17 shows that there is no direct correlation between the *number* of TMs and the predominance of TMs other than *na.*

Table 1
Contexts of the PS and FS data samples.

Speaker	Variety	Age/Sex	First Language	Discourse Type	Total Number of Distinct TMs Used in All Discourse
Z	PS	26f	Somali	autobiography	2
G	PS	38m	Gujerati	personal narrative	4
B	PS	24	Somali	converse w PS spkrs	4
H	PS	43m	Arabic	anecdotes	5
MJ	For. Talk[9]	61m	FS	conv w new spkr	4
J	Out-Talk[9]	16m	FS	conv w non-FS spkr	7
J	In-Talk[9]	16m	FS	conv w FS spkrs	8

Table 2

Elaboration of the TM system in spoken discourse.

Speaker	Status	Percent of TMs Used Other Than NA	Total Number of Occurrences of All TMs	Total Number of Distinct TMs Used in All Discourse
Z	PS	0	40	2
G	PS	11	53	4
B	PS	42	24	4
H	PS	16	85	5
MJ	For. Talk	16	63	4
J	FS-o	47	87	7
J	FS-i	98	284	8

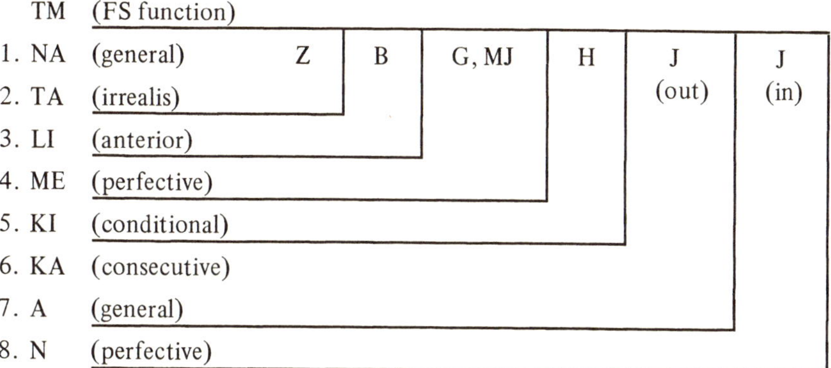

Figure 1

Common ordering of the TM paradigm for PS and FS speakers.

Only J's in-talk shows a pattern in which *na* is no longer the most frequent TM. This is typical of the vernacular style of FS in Mombasa. Table 3 below shows that when *na* and *a* are considered together, they virtually reverse frequency according to style whereby *na* becomes extremely rare in the vernacular style.

Table 3

Percentage of *na* out of *na* and *a* together for J's two styles of speech.

	Out-Talk	In-Talk
Percent of *na*	96	11
Percent of *na* out of total number of *na* + *a*	47	42

The high favorability of *na* to PS discourses indicates that it retains its general pidgin use as an all-purpose marker unrelated to distinction in tense and aspect through depidginization. This remains the case in Foreigner Talk. In out-talk, *na* remains the most frequent TM. *Na* and *a* together account for 54 percent of J's out-talk TMs. In in-talk, *na* and *a* are reduced to 15 percent of all TMs used. This shows that even in the fluent out-talk style, *na* is of more general use than both *na* and *a* together are in the vernacular, although its generality is not as extreme as for most PS speakers.

The preceding evidence indicates that the general TM, *na*, in PS is a possible substitute for all other TMs in all varieties of Swahili short of the vernacular. In depidginization, TMs other than *na* replace it to some extent, but it continues to function as an all-purpose marker. This function of *na* is echoed in Foreigner Talk and even to a great extent in the out-talk style of FS. This means that if PS speakers aim at an FS out-talk target, the FS style most likely to be addressed to them—some of the PS usage of *na*, with which they are already familiar—will be reflected back to them.

5. The SM in depidginization. The SM obligatorily precedes the TM marked verb in FS, but is unknown in PS. Concurrent with the elaboration of the TM system in depidginization is the development of SM marking. The SM occurs as a variable category for the four PS speakers.

The speakers differ in the variety and consistency of the SMs used. Whereas FS contains a concordial SM paradigm of 25 SMs—6 personal SMs (three each singular and plural) and 19 inanimate noun classes (both singular and plural)—no PS speaker used anywhere near all of these.

The general depidginizing pattern is to distinguish the personal (animate) SM paradigm from an inanimate SM *i-* (adapted from FS Class 9). An interesting rudimentary pattern was used by G. He adapted the SM *u-* (FS 2sg) as a general animate SM as opposed to *i-* for any inanimate. G used *u-* for the 1pl (FS *tu-*) twice and once for the 3sg (FS *a-*) as in the following examples:

/7/ nne–saa–nusu–si–na-sunguka–ku-vua–samaki.–wakati–na-pata
u-me-pata–nne–pamoja
four–hour–half–we–TM-round–inf-catch–fish.–time–TM-get
SM-Perf-get–four–together
"We sailed around fishing for four and a half hours. When we got (one), we got four together."

(G:38m, Gujerati)

In /7/ the first two finite verbs are unmarked. The third is marked with the SM *u-* referring to 'we'.

/8/ alafu–sis–na-stuka–hii–maneno–iko–namna–gani–paka–bwana–
u-me-kasirika
then–we–TM-shock–this–words–cop–way–what–until–husband–
SM-Perf-anger
"Then we were startled by this kind of talk (by the wife) until the husband got mad."

(G:38m, Gujerati)

In /8/ the SM *u-* refers to a third singular subject, 'husband'.

The other speakers used the personal SMs according to the FS norms on the rare occasions that they used them at all, e.g., H used the animate 3sg *a-* eight times and 3pl *wa-* once in addition to the inanimate *i-* (four times).

The form of the SM is properly a concordial matter. In studying SM variation here we will only be concerned with whether the SM category is used at all, regardless of whether its form agrees with FS concordial usage. In coding the variation between use and nonuse of the SM, two constructions were excluded from consideration in which PS does not differ from FS in surface SM absence:

a. The 1sg SM *ni-* before the TM *na:* in FS *ni-na-* reduces to *na-* almost categorically through degemination of an intermediate condensation *n-na* caused by nasal syllabification.

b. Any vocalic SM following a word ending in an identical vowel is most often perceptually identical to SM absence due to identical vowel reduction. This is most commonly the case with the 3sg SM *a-* following . . . *a ##*.

Table 4 on p. 21 displays the SM marking behavior of the speakers.[10] Both PS and Foreigner Talk show variable SM marking, but both fluent sytles of FS show categorical use of the FS norm.

6. Covariation of SM marking with TM elaboration. Figure 2 on p. 22 shows that for PS speakers there is a close correlation between the percentage of SM marking and TM elaboration. The greater the percentage of TMs other than *na* used in discourse, the greater the use of the SM. This indicates that elaboration of the TM system and SM marking are acquired concurrently, both as adoptions from the FS system.

By contrast, Foreigner Talk is discernible as an FS style rather than a PS type by the high rate of SM marking despite the low rate of use of TMs other than *na*. It is reasonable to assume that FS speakers would have difficulty in suppressing SM marking due to its frequent and automatic use in more fluent styles.

A final pattern of great interest distinguishes SM marking behavior for *na* as opposed to the other TMs in PS and Foreigner Talk. Table 5 on p. 21 shows that *na* resists SM marking to a much greater degree than the other TMs for PS speakers, and that Foreigner Talk fits this pattern.

This discontinuity in SM marking according to TM shows up in Figure 3, p. 22, as a considerable gap between the lines representing differential rates of SM marking with *na* and with the other TMs.

The two lines in the pattern of Figure 3 are suggestive of a separation between: 1) the basic PS pattern consisting of Ø (i.e., no) SM marking and the invariant use of *na;* and 2) the FS pattern consisting of SM marking and a multiple system of TMs. In the concluding section, we will discuss to what extent this pattern can be considered part of a single grammatical system and what this reveals about the nature of depidginization of PS in Coastal Kenya.

7. Conclusions. The existence of a stable PS grammar allows us to recognize the source of one set of features in the depidginizing speech of PS speakers. The two relevant norms are Ø SM marking and *na* as the unique TM. On these points PS differs from fluent FS, which has obligatory SM marking and an elaborate TM system. The combinations of the conflicting PS and FS norms can be analyzed into two separate variables as identified in /9/ below:

/9/	Variable	FS Norm	PS Norm
	(SM)	SM	Ø
	(TM)	TM	NA

The FS norm TM represents the entire set of TMs for FS speakers and any multiple TM set used by PS speakers. As we have seen, TM includes *na* for FS speakers but is sharply graded in frequency according to style from a maximum

Table 4
Total frequencies of SM marking in spoken discourse.

Speaker	Status	Percent of SMs per Number of TMs	Total Number of Occurrences of TMs
Z	PS	3	40
G	PS	8	53
B	PS	63	24
H	PS	15	85
MJ	For. Talk	54	63
J	FS-o	100	87
J	FS-i	100	284

Table 5
Rate of SM marking by TM (NA : non-NA) for spoken discourse.

Speaker	Status	TM	SM	Ø SM	% SM
Z	PS	NA	1	39	3
		non-NA	–	–	–
G	PS	NA	0	47	0
		non-NA	4	2	67
B	PS	NA	5	9	36
		non-NA	10	0	100
H	PS	NA	7	64	10
		non-NA	6	8	43
MJ	For. Talk	NA	25	28	47
		non-NA	9	1	90

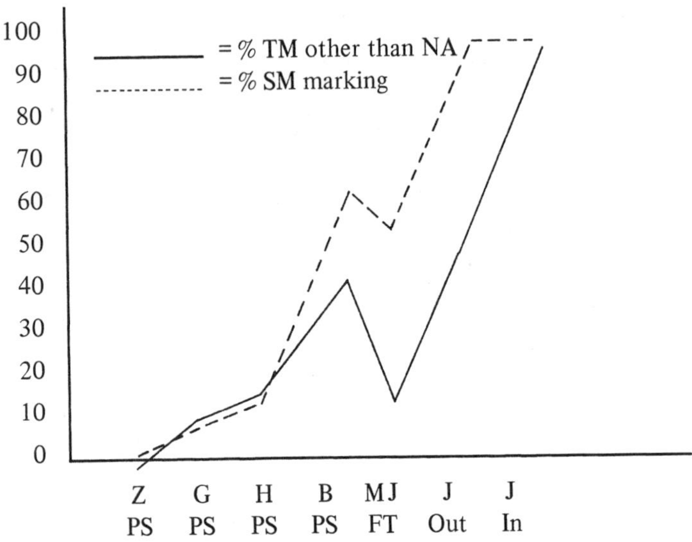

Figure 2
Correlation of TM elaboration and SM marking for PS and FS speakers.

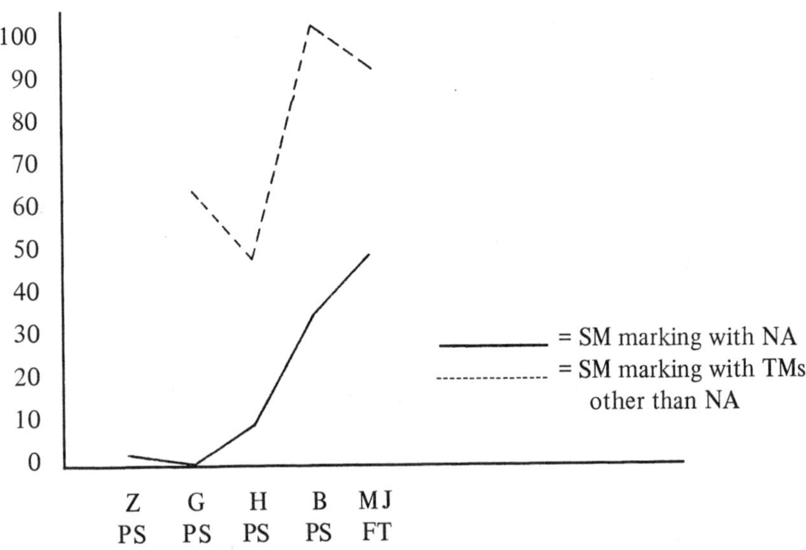

Figure 3
Discontinuity between SM marking with NA and with other TMs for PS and FT.

in Foreigner Talk to a minimum in the vernacular. For PS speakers we consider *na* to be separate from all other TMs (except *ma* for H) so that the variable (TM) represents variation between *na* on the one hand and all other TMs on the other.

From a language independent point of view, there is no necessary relationship between the two distinct syntactic processes of SM marking and TM elaboration. Nevertheless, we see covariation in depidginization between the two variables (TM) and (SM), as discussed in the preceding section.

The depidginizing PS does not accurately fit a diglossic model of the type in /10/ below:

/10/ a. ∅, NA *c. SM, NA
b. SM, TM *d. ∅, TM

Neither combination /10c/ nor /10d/ is excluded in depidginization. Both simply occur more rarely than /10a/ and /10b/.

A polylectal analysis of the type in /11/ below:

/11/ a. ∅, NA c. SM, NA
b. SM, TM *d. ∅, TM

placing /11c/ as a system intermediate between /11a/ and /11b/, is appropriate for describing the range of FS from a basilectal Foreigner Talk to the acrolectal styles of FS, if the one example of /11d/, as opposed to nine examples of /11b/ for MJ, is discounted as insignificant and therefore unsystematic. However, for depidginization (as opposed to a "denativization" of Foreigner Talk) as seen in Figure 3, p. 22, covariation between variable (SM) and (TM) works the same way although at discontinuously large rates.

The variable rule model of Labov (1972a) allows us to express all the depidginizing relationships in a single rule of the type illustrated in /12/:

/12/ $\emptyset \rightarrow \langle \text{SM} \rangle \quad / \quad \_\_\_\_ \; \# \; \langle -\text{NA} \rangle$

by which ⟨ –NA ⟩, i.e., other TMs, are more favorable to SM marking than *na,* but that all TMs including *na* allow SM marking. This form of description has the virtue of allowing precise comparison with the obligatory FS rule of SM marking which is given in /13/ below:

/13/ $\emptyset \rightarrow \text{SM} \quad / \quad \_\_\_\_ \; \# \; \text{TM}$

an approximation of the FS target. However, when we consider motivation for a rule like /12/, the only plausible reason to single out *na* from other TMs is because it is the general pidgin TM. In PS it is associated with Ø SM, equivalent to non-operation of rule /12/. In depidginization this association continues to exert an influence. Since it is the pidgin origin of *na* that shapes rule /12/ rather than its morphological form or grammatical function, reformulation of rule /12/ as /14/ is more explanatory:

/14/ Ø → ⟨ SM ⟩ / ___ # ⟨ –Pidgin ⟩

Now, in view of the pidgin origin of *na* and the associated lack of SM, we cannot consider rule /12/ or /14/ to represent a *single* intermediate system, since [Pidgin] refers to a distinctive system itself. More plausibly, the rule indicates an intermediate stage in the reconciliation of two distinct systems: PS, already acquired and laying the foundation for depidginization; and FS, the new target.

To return to the initial theme of this paper, depidginizing PS speakers show by their speech behavior a distinct separation of PS and FS as independent sets of features, and yet PS acts as a basis, or "bridge," for acquiring the more elaborate structures of FS. The unique TM *na* at once provides a category from which to elaborate the TM paradigm of FS and a structure to which FS SM marking can be prefixed. It is not at all suggested that PS evolved for this purpose. The point is that PS is *available* for this purpose and thus presents a case of a pidgin which can be used as a medium for the acquisition of a vernacular language as well as for communication among heterogeneous non-first language speakers. How widespread this phenomenon is in multilingual situations, including cases where no pidgin has yet been proposed to mediate between one first language and another first language vernacular target, remains for further study.

NOTES

1. The 1969 Kenya population census materials do not directly present population by first language. Usually first language can be identified by ethnic group, but in the case of Swahili in Mombasa, sizable numbers of FS speakers are distributed among the Arab and Bajun (5 percent and 2 percent of total Mombasa population, respectively) populations. A small, but undetermined, number of ethnic groups originating outside Mombasa speak FS, but even being born in Mombasa does not insure that Swahili rather than the ethnic language will be acquired first. Another limitation on interpreting the census materials is that inter-ethnic people are not recorded; according to local custom, they are assigned

to a particular ethnic group, e.g., the father in the case of Arabs. Inter-ethnic people in Mombasa are likely to be FS speakers regardless of the background of their parents.

2. A secondary reason that PS speakers express negative attitudes toward their speech is that it is distinct from Standard Swahili. This identification reflects the lack of the status symbol of education in the use of PS, an economic rather than an ethnic symbol, but one far inferior to the economic symbolism associated with the use of English (cf. Scotton 1976).

3. Aural teaching of translation of words and phrases does exist in nature. I personally witnessed a session in which a new learner was exercised by an uneducated PS speaker in translating the phrase "I gave you five shillings. Where is my change?" from Somali to Swahili. Revealingly, the phrase *na-KU-pa* 'I give you' offered by the new speaker, probably coincidentally resembling the FS norm, was "corrected" by the PS speaker to *na-Mpa,* where *mpa* is the unanalyzed verb 'give' in PS, but a complex structure *m* (OM = him) *-pa* (give) in FS: *na-mpa* 'I give' in PS is formally identical to FS *na-m-pa* 'I give him/her'.

4. Following quotations, social information about the speaker is given in the form (initial[s] of first name, age, sex, first language).

5. On the other hand, the difference in word order between the PS sentence and its FS equivalent reflects the influence of the speaker's Somali, an SOV language. Before overrating this distinction, it must be noted that although FS and some varieties of PS tend to be SVO like English or Spanish, FS allows great freedom in word order so that in some contexts SOV, etc., are admissible and even preferred.

6. In FS *-ko* is used strictly as a locative-existential copula, never as an equative copula, and is obligatorily SM marked; *i-*, only for Class 9 subject; and *yu-*, for Class 1 subjects (animate singular). In PS these morphemes are unanalyzed but reveal different grammatical sources chosen for stereotyping in the two PS varieties.

7. An atrocious grammatical description by Carcoforo (1935) of Swahili spoken in Benadir (Southern Somalia) exemplifies some Northern PS norms. Although he ignores prior scholarship, does not identify his sources, uses Italian orthography, and allows more than occasional misprints, frequent examples of the use of *ma* and *yuko* (see text) in Northern PS appear in the section "Racolti di frasi e dialoghi," possibly obtained as translations from Italian by Somali PS speakers. In Carcoforo, *ma* occurs as a variant of *me* rather than *na,* although *ma* is never mentioned in his section on the TMs. Observed Northern PS speakers do not distinguish *ma* and *na,* and the system remains one of a single TM.

8. One is tempted to argue that one cannot be sure of the total inventory of TMs used by the speakers on the basis of limited data. This is true but not to the point here for two reasons. First, PS speakers in Mombasa have a passive knowl-

ledge of all the TMs of FS in form if not in function, but apparently find them generally unnecessary for their communicative purposes. Secondly, on extremely rare occasions a structure with a further TM occurs for some speakers, but because they are so rare it would be difficult to maintain that they are systematic or productive regardless of whether they are analyzed as distinct morphemes by the speakers.

9. Foreigner Talk is the style or register used by FS speakers to new learners of Swahili displaying minimal competence in the language. Out-talk is the style used generally to noncommunity members, whether PS speakers or of greater approximation to FS. In-talk, or the vernacular, is used largely with FS community members and other familiars who may not be coethnic (see Wald [1973] for detailed discussion).

10. In Table 4, H's *ma* has not been included in the count. *Ma* turned out to exclude SM marking invariably, and thus does not participate in any pattern of covariation between SM marking and TM marking.

DECREOLIZATION IN A CREOLE CONTINUUM: BELIZE[1]

Genevieve Escure
University of Minnesota

This paper is a pilot study of the patterning of the decreolization process as observed in intra-group situations among Belizean Creoles.[2] A combination of linguistic features, both phonological and morphosyntactic, has been selected[3] in order to test linguistic variability along the continuum. The motivation behind this approach is twofold. First, it determines which of the linguistic features investigated constitute reliable cues to the variability, and more specifically, to the process of decreolization, or deviation from a creole norm. Then further research can focus on the detailed analysis of the most significant cues. Second, a comparison of the respective indicator values of phonological and syntactic features is intended. Previous sociolinguistic studies have found that linguistic gradata are often characterized by sharp syntactic stratification vs. gradient phonological stratification (Labov 1972b; Shuy, Wolfram and Riley 1967). The case study of Belize will demonstrate whether such discrepancy in the variability of linguistic features obtains in the Belizean continuum.

Methodology

The relative value of linguistic cues has been assessed by means of quantitative analysis. All samples examined involved fifteen to twenty minutes of taped segments recorded in various contextual situations by a native fieldworker.[4] Tables 1a and 2a (pp. 28 and 30) show the actual raw frequencies associated with phonological and syntactic cues, respectively; and Tables 1b and 2b (pp. 29 and 31) display corresponding percentages. Nonsignificant cues have been eliminated from Tables 1b and 2b. A given feature is defined as nonsignificant if its incidence is extremely low, that is, if the potential occurrences of this feature are less than five in the majority of the cells. Some features are still considered significant if only a few cells contain less than five potential occurrences. In this case, the low incidence cell is left blank, and thus not incorporated in the calculation of the mean of a given sample (shown to the extreme right), or in the mean of a linguistic feature (shown below the table).

The Continuum in Belize

Decreolization has been defined as a phenomenon which takes place when "a creole is in the process of merging with the standard" (DeCamp 1971) and thus

Table 1a
PHONOLOGICAL CUES: Raw Frequencies

Speakers	CC / C	ʌ / ɔ	ɔ / a	aw / o	ə / o a	ir / ɛ	ð / d	θ / t	oy / ay
1. Errol/D	8/8	6/6	5/5	9/9	5/5	3/3	5/5	4/4	1/1
2. Dudu	10/10	6/6	8/8	8/8	18/18	6/6	7/7	5/5	4/4
3. Toni	12/12	6/6	3/3	5/5	7/7	3/3	6/6	3/3	1/1
4. Sonia/X	5/5	2/2	4/4	5/5	8/8	3/3	9/10	3/4	2/2
5. Blink	11/11	8/8	13/13	10/10	15/15	8/8	16/18	7/11	9/9
6. Philip	6/6	3/3	7/7	6/6	5/5	2/2	6/7	5/8	4/4
7. Andrew	3/3	10/10	5/5	5/5	4/5	2/3	12/13	11/15	0/0
8. Errol/K	9/9	7/8	11/11	7/8	5/5	3/3	5/6	4/6	0/0
9. Doris	4/4	4/4	10/11	15/15	6/9	5/6	9/10	3/4	2/2
10. Lucille	10/10	7/7	8/8	8/10	6/8	2/5	4/6	2/5	2/2
11. Sonia/E	10/10	9/11	9/9	10/10	10/12	5/6	3/6	5/13	2/2
12. Karim	12/12	3/3	9/13	4/5	2/4	4/5	9/12	5/7	2/2
13. Tensy	15/16	3/4	13/20	8/11	5/11	2/7	9/20	1/3	0/0
14. Eddie	3/3	1/3	4/4	6/9	10/12	1/2	4/9	0/3	1/2
15. Errol/X	4/4	2/4	3/4	3/4	5/8	1/2	5/10	6/11	0/0
16. Peter	11/13	11/21	14/22	8/16	10/26	6/7	8/13	4/16	0/3
17. Flowers	9/10	1/3	3/7	0/10	2/9	0/4	0/9	0/6	0/2

Table 1b
PHONOLOGICAL CUES: Percentages

Speakers	CC | C	ʌ | ɔ	ɔ | a	aw | o	ə /\ o a	ð | d	θ | t	Sample Mean
1. Errol/D	1.00	1.00	1.00	1.00	1.00	1.00		1.00
2. Dudu	1.00	1.00	1.00	1.00	1.00	1.00	1.00	1.00
3. Toni	1.00	1.00		1.00	1.00	1.00		1.00
4. Sonia/X	1.00			1.00	1.00	.90		.97
5. Blink	1.00	1.00	1.00	1.00	1.00	.89	.64	.93
6. Philip	1.00		1.00	1.00	1.00	.86	.62	.91
7. Andrew		1.00	1.00	1.00	.80	.92	.73	.91
8. Errol/K	1.00	.87	1.00	.87	1.00	.83	.67	.89
9. Doris			.91	1.00	.67	.90		.87
10. Lucille	1.00	1.00	1.00	.80	.75	.67	.40	.80
11. Sonia/E	1.00	.82	1.00	1.00	.83	.50	.38	.79
12. Karim	1.00		.69	.80		.75	.71	.79
13. Tensy	.94		.90	.73	.45	.45		.69
14. Eddie				.67	.83	.44		.65
15. Errol/X					.62	.50	.55	.56
16. Peter	.85	.52	.64	.50	.38	.62	.25	.54
17. Flowers	.90		.43	.0	.22	.0	.0	.26
Feature Mean	.98	.91	.89	.84	.78	.72	.54	.80
								.81

Table 2a
SYNTACTIC CUES: Raw Frequencies

Speakers	∅ 3sg	∅ Poss	∅ Past	∅ DoNeg	∅ Cop	∅ Pl	De	Me	Fi
1. Errol/D	2/2	2/2	2/2	8/8	10/10	7/9	3/3	2/2	1/1
2. Dudu/E	5/5	1/1	9/9	13/13	4/4	7/11	5/5	1/1	1/1
3. Toni/E	9/9	0/0	2/2	2/2	4/4	1/5	4/4	1/1	0/0
4. Sonia/X	1/1	1/1	0/0	3/3	7/7	1/4	3/3	4/4	1/1
5. Blink	5/5	3/3	30/45	11/15	10/13	22/37	12/15	15/45	0/3
6. Philip	1/1	0/0	2/3	0/0	4/4	1/2	2/2	2/2	0/0
7. Andrew	5/5	1/1	10/10	3/3	3/3	3/5	4/4	5/5	1/1
8. Errol/K	8/12	2/2	2/3	3/3	5/8	8/16	0/2	0/3	0/2
9. Doris	9/9	2/2	19/26	8/11	8/23	4/15	9/23	0/5	0/1
10. Lucille	1/1	0/0	10/13	6/8	6/11	6/7	3/9	0/3	0/1
11. Sonia/E	5/5	0/0	2/2	6/13	4/11	3/13	0/11	0/5	0/1
12. Karim	3/5	0/0	10/10	3/6	7/8	4/19	0/5	0/9	0/3
13. Tensy	7/8	4/5	9/41	7/13	3/12	10/23	2/21	0/49	0/6
14. Eddie	2/4	0/1	2/5	0/2	0/4	2/17	0/2	0/3	0/2
15. Errol	0/1	0/1	0/6	1/11	0/6	1/12	0/5	0/4	0/2
16. Peter	19/32	3/3	4/12	2/19	5/15	2/36	1/15	0/20	0/1
17. Flowers	1/3	0/4	0/7	0/8	0/10	3/16	0/10	0/4	0/2

Table 2b
SYNTACTIC CUES: Percentages

Speakers	Ø 3sg	Ø Past	Ø DoNeg	Ø Cop	Ø Pl	De	Sample Mean
1. Errol/D			1.00	1.00	.78		.93
2. Dudu/E	1.00	1.00	1.00		.64	1.00	.93
3. Toni/E	1.00				.20		.60
4. Sonia/X				1.00			
5. Blink	1.00	.67	.73	.77	.59	.80	.76
6. Philip							
7. Andrew	1.00	1.00			.60		.87
8. Errol/K	.67			.62	.50		.60
9. Doris	1.00	.73	.73	.35	.27	.39	.58
10. Lucille		.77	.75	.55	.86	.33	.65
11. Sonia/E	1.00		.46	.36	.23	.0	.41
12. Karim	.60	1.00	.50	.87	.21	.0	.53
13. Tensy	.87	.22	.54	.25	.43	.10	.40
14. Eddie		.40			.12		.26
15. Errol/X		.0	.09	.0	.08	.0	.03
16. Peter	.59	.33	.11	.33	.05	.07	.25
17. Flowers		.0	.0	.0	.19	.0	.04
Feature Mean	.87	.57	.54	.51	.38	.27	.52
							.52

characterizes so-called post-creole continua like the Jamaican continuum. The implication of this interpretation of decreolization has often been that the fully creolized (or basilectal) end of the continuum becomes lost as simultaneously the mesolectal (intermediate) varieties keep expanding in the direction of the target language (or acrolect).[5] Bickerton (1975) interprets decreolization as part of a learning process according to which new generations of Guyanese speakers learn more Anglicized versions of the old creole. His study and others describe speakers whose variability performance is limited to a relatively narrow range of the continuum; that is, there are distinct basilectal, mesolectal, and acrolectal speakers–the acrolectal users being typically members of a higher socioeconomic class (Bickerton 1975).

The case study of Belize, as assessed at this early stage of the investigation, indicates that decreolization is an individual phenomenon which is primarily related to contextual situations. Most speakers of the community under investigation control a complex linguistic repertoire, including basilectal and mesolectal, as well as acrolectal, varieties, and develop the ability to switch between codes and variants when appropriate without abandoning their native creole variety.[6] Belizeans commonly perceive three discrete segments within the continuum, namely, "raw creole" or "broad creole" (the basilect), "broken English" (the mesolect), and English (the acrolect), which is in fact a West Indian standard.

The decreolization process is statistically analyzed as deviation from a creole norm, "raw creole" being the native language used by all speakers in this population sample (see the Appendix, p. 39, for informant data). All features selected are characteristic of the basilect which ideally includes in its most stable state maximal frequencies of creole features. Then the lower the figures, the closer one gets to the acrolectal pole, i.e., English.

Variability of Phonological Features

Nine phonological features have been examined in a variety of contextual situations, all spontaneously elicited. They include:

CC—C : lack of consonant clusters, as in *next* [nɛs] ; *first* [fɔs]

Λ—ɔ : rounded reflex of English /Λ/ and /ṛ/ as in *duck* [dɔk] ; *bunk* [bɔ̃k] ; *drum* [drɔ̃] ; *bird* [bɔ:d]

ɔ—a : unrounded reflex of the English lowback vowel, as in *law* [la] ; *small* [smal] ; *call* [kal]

aw—o : midback vowel as reflex of English diphthong /aw/, as in *house* [hos] ; *now* [no] ; *town* [tõ]

ə—o/a : colored value of vowels not bearing primary stress, as in *water* [wata] ; *funeral* [fyuneral] ; *pressure* [preša] ir–ϵ : lowmid reflex of the English highfront vowel before /r/; besides, /r/ is rarely realized, or surfaces as a coronal glide, as in *beer* [bϵ] or [bϵə]; *hear, here* [hϵ]; *pier* [pϵ]; *near* [nϵ]

ð–d : noncontinuant reflex of the English voiced interdental, as in *that* [dat]; *weather* [weda]; *brother* [breda]

θ–t : noncontinuant reflex of the English voiceless interdental, as in *thin* [tin]; *think* [tik]; *North* [nat]

oy–ay : low onset of the English diphthong /oy/, as in *boy* [bway]; *oil* [ayl]; *enjoy* [inǰay]; *choice* [čays]

Of the nine features tested in Table 1a (p. 28), only seven have been retained in Table 1b (p. 29), since the features /ir–ϵ/ and /oy–ay/ do not occur in a sufficient number of cases. In the rare occurrences of items containing /oy–ay/, e.g., *boil, choice* (*boy* is the only frequent item of this kind), /ay/ is practically always the variant produced, and is thus not identified as stigmatized at any point on the continuum. The same holds true for the feature /ir–ϵ/.

It is significant to note that the range of phonological variation represented in Table 1b (p. 29) is relatively narrow, between 1.0 and .80 for two-thirds of the speakers, with an overall mean of .80 across samples and .81 across features. Creole phonetic variants predominate throughout the continuum, which is represented by the cross section of samples 1 through 17. Sample 17 is the only one to evidence a fairly important degree of decreolization with a sample mean of .26. The context is formal (a church meeting), which triggers the loss of at least a few basilectal features. However, notice the almost total absence of consonant clusters (.90), and the still significant unrounding of /ɔ/ (.43). The classroom situation (sample 14) involves only moderate phonological decreolization (.65), even though it constitutes a linguistically formal situation in which "raw creole" is not relevant. Thus, the continuum as observed in Placencia, Belize, seems to be characterized by an overall standardization of creole phonological features. Typically, creole sound patterns, e.g., [hϵ] for *here,* [tõ] for *town,* are not, or are perhaps no longer, stigmatized.[7] The seven features shown in Table 1b (p. 29) evidence only slight differential behavior in their sensitivity to the overall decreolization process. In nonbasilectal contexts speakers clearly introduce interdentals before they introduce consonant clusters. In fact, hardly any speaker produces clusters even in the most acrolectal varieties, as indicated by the feature mean of .98. As far as interdentals are concerned, the .54 feature mean associated with /θ–t/ indicates that the noncontinuant variant (*thin* pronounced [tin], for example) is somewhat stigmatized in acrolectal samples, and is much more so than its voiced counterpart /ð–d/, which averages .72.

Furthermore, the decreolization of phonological features is very gradual within its narrow range, as can be seen by looking at the span covered by the continuum of the samples examined. Cells are generally implicationally arranged, with the exception of a few deviant cells, and this holds across samples as well as across features.

Variability of Morphosyntactic Features

The nine features investigated include:

Ø 3sg Nonmarking of third person singular present:

1. i laik it
   'he likes it'

Ø Poss Nonmarking of possessive case:

2. mai mada breda
   'my mother's brother'
3. di shark bait of mai li breda flesh
   'the shark bit off (a piece of) my little brother's flesh'

Ø Past Nonmarking of strong preterites:

4. i gaan en i fain nobadi
   'he went and found nobody'
5. i ron til no de sait
   'he ran until he was out of sight'

Ø DoNeg Absence of auxiliary 'do' in negative sentences:

6. in no waan it
   'he doesn't want it'
7. i no kom bak eni mor
   'he didn't come back anymore'

Ø Cop Absence of the copula 'be' before stative verbs (adjectives):

8. i bex
   'she is mad!'
9. dat sopoz to daan, tu finish laang taim
   'that's supposed to have been done, to have been finished a long time ago'

Ø Pl Nonmarking of plural:

10. tu bwai
    'two boys'
11. ho moch man?
    'how many men?'

de Continuative, locative, or iterative marker:

12. Bra Anansi de plan tu go tiif ya hag
    'Bra Anansi is planning to go steal a pig'

13. wa de ga an?
    'what's going on?'
14. Bra Fayaflai de da staan, Bra Anansi de da bo
    'Bra Firefly is at the stern, Bra Anansi is at the bow'
15. di chilin jos go ron e de ful
    'the children just keep running and fooling around'

me Anterior or simple past marker:

16. a me tink faiv hondred da me di arenjmint
    'I thought that five hundred was the arrangement'
17. a me bex bika a me pas di ting, e neva ivon si it
    'I was mad because I had passed the thing, and didn't even see it'

fi Possessive marker attached to the possessor, provided the latter is not a long NP:

18. fi-yu wata naisa a fi-wi wan, we wi ga da fi-mi hos
    'your water is nicer than ours, that we got in my house'

Three features have been removed from Table 2b (p. 31) because of their low incidence. They are: /∅ Poss/, /me/, and /fi/. Typically, possessive contexts are not widespread. As for the feature /me/, it happens to be scarce in the samples analyzed (except sample 5) simply because the conversations from which those samples were drawn included few past tense references. The six remaining significant cues shown in Table 2b can be divided into two categories: cues such as /∅ 3sg/, /∅ Past/, /∅ DoNeg/, /∅ Cop/, and /∅ Pl/ all reflect the *absence* of English morphological markers; /de/ is in a separate category since it is a basilectal marker and is quantified to represent the *presence* of a creole marker (had /me/ and /fi/ had a higher incidence, they would have belonged to this category).

The range of morphosyntactic variability is significantly wider than the deviation from creole phonological patterns observed above. The range represented in Table 2b is quite important–from .93 for the most basilectal samples to .04 for the upper acrolectal varieties. The overall syntactic decreolization mean (across samples) is .52 as opposed to the .80 phonological decreolization index indicated in Table 1b (p. 29). This clearly implies that creole morphosyntactic features are stigmatized in more formal though still natural and spontaneous contexts. Particularly striking is the almost total absence of creole features observed in the acrolectal segment of the linguistic spectrum, i.e., roughly, samples 14 through 17. English markers are nonexistent in "raw creole" but are increasingly inserted as the varieties approach the official standard.[8] The cue /∅ Pl/ is an exception in that some degree of plural marking occurs even in the most basilectal varieties and gradually increases toward the acrolectal samples. Increase in plural marking means of course decreolization of the /∅ Pl/ feature. The categorical component of plural marking is related to syllable structure: items with a stem-final non-consonantal segment are always marked (e.g., [mãgoz] *mangoes;* [kiz] *keys* 'islands'; [pyepaz] *papers*), with the exception of *boys,* usually realized as [bway]. Decreolization of /∅Pl/ indicates some degree of plural marking after consonantal segments. Some of the English and creole morphemes have similar, though not identical, functions. Thus, to remain consistent with the interpretation of decreolization as departure from the creole norm, all six features have been defined in terms of their respective semantactic functions in the creole system, as based on a prior analysis of the morphemes in question in "raw creole." Some creole and zero-English morphemes occur in complementary distribution in the basilect but may have overlapping domains in other varieties. This is the case for /de/ and /∅Cop/. As indicated above, /de/ as creole copula has a specific domain of occurrence as a continuative, locative, and iterative marker. However, /de/ is in complementary distribution in the basilectal system with /∅Cop/ which occurs in attributive position before adjectives (or stative verbs) and nonlocative adverbials. A special relationship thus holds between /∅Cop/ and /de/, but the syntactic conditions of occurrence of these two morphemes become blurred in mesolectal varieties, as the English /be/ copula increasingly spreads in the positions occupied in the basilect by /∅Cop/ and /de/, respectively.[9] Thus, /de/ as a creole marker typically designates a variety as either basilectal or nonbasilectal, whereas all other morphemes function variably, approximating in subtle ways the target language, English. All four features–/∅3sg/, /∅Past/, /∅DoNeg/, and /∅Cop/–exhibit maximal figures in "raw creole," but show fine stratification in the nonbasilectal varieties, and in particular in the intermediate varieties. There is a gradual but steady increase in irregular preterites, auxiliary-plus-negative forms, and copulas whenever a speaker intends to switch away from "raw creole," and the three features are almost consistently realized as English markers in acrolectal varieties. However, the third person singular of the present tense remains largely unmarked, except in upper mesolectal and acrolectal samples (samples 12 through 17). The feature averages shown at the bottom of Table 2b (p. 31) illustrate the differential decreolization of the five features, ranging from .87 (for /∅3sg/) to .27 (for /de/). The three intermediate cues–/∅Past/, /∅DoNeg/, and /∅Cop/–which constitute the best indicators of the variety level achieved in a given sample, exhibit comparable averages of .57, .54, and .51, respectively.

Thus, intra-group communication evidences great linguistic flexibility, at least as far as grammatical features are concerned. But the phonological component undergoes comparatively little variability across the linguistic spectrum since creole sound patterns are not stigmatized to the extent that creole morphosyntactic features are. Such discrepancy is not surprising, considering that children are taught English in school primarily as a reading and writing tool, and creole remains the pragmatic medium of oral communication. Creole speakers thus learn to distinguish between English and creole grammatical features, but are never systematically made aware of potential phonological differences. The differential decreolization observable in the phonological and syntactic components is, therefore, determined during early school years, thus inevitably entailing a certain overlap of the native language (creole) and the second language (English). However, school and government policies intent on imposing English as the only literate or educated language are counteracted by various other influences internal to the community. There is a double standard inherent in all creole communities. Creole is avoided for external contacts, but it is internally prestigious. It is unmistakably the spontaneous medium in peer group and family contacts. Those few individuals who leave the community for the United States, for example, and return having "forgotten" the local vernacular, sporting a Black English variety instead, are laughed at as "taakin amerikan." The acrolect is usually appropriate only when talking to outsiders, and in particular to government officials, mostly because those officials also choose to speak English as a status symbol. In native formal situations, "broken English" is preferred; these situations include: village council meetings, church meetings or parties, and any conversation involving serious topics. For instance, an old woman discussing with her grandson (the interviewer) the historical background of the village founding and the related involvement of family members consistently used a mesolectal variety in spite of the fact that the fieldworker intentionally spoke creole; she was obviously aware of her role as historian, and somehow directed her story to the outside world, and produced an appropriate code. Yet the acrolect would have been too stilted to fit a private conversation with her grandson.

The comparative analysis of the Belizean continuum in terms of a few phonological and morphosyntactic features has shown that decreolization affects grammatical rather than phonological elements in the continuum. In addition, decreolization can be understood as the consequence of conflicting pressures inherent in the Placencia community and, more specifically, the tension between external language policy and the internal vitality of the vernacular. Such conflicts exist in all speech communities to a certain extent but are particularly well illustrated in creole communities. The mesolectal set of varieties resulting from the interaction of the creole and English systems constitutes an extremely complex area which is far from being understood, and must be left to further investigation.

NOTES

1. Research was supported by a University of Minnesota Graduate School grant.

2. There are five major ethnic groups in Belize that have preserved distinct native languages. Creoles (of Afro-European descent) represent about 31 percent of the population and are native speakers of Belizean Creole (English-based) which often functions as the lingua franca in interaction among different ethnic groups.

3. Feature selection has been effected on the basis of preliminary observations made in the summer of 1977, and six months of fieldwork done in 1978 in Placencia, a fishing village (population 400) located in the southern Stann Creek district.

4. Contexts range from formal to informal, including official situations such as village council meetings and church meetings, as well as peer group and family conversations. Tape-recorded sessions were conducted with the help of, or exclusively by, a native Creole fieldworker trained in interviewing procedures. All samples analyzed were elicited in spontaneous situations.

5. The terms "basilect," "mesolect," and "acrolect" have been regularly used in recent creole studies, and are used here for convenient reference with no value judgments implied; indeed, none of these three segments can be consistently labeled as stigmatized, or prestigious.

6. It is, of course, not excluded that one end of the continuum will eventually disappear. Some creole lexical items are indeed in the process of becoming lost in Belizean Creole (e.g., *nyam* is being replaced by *eat*).

7. See Escure (1978) for examples of homophonous pairs, and a general discussion of the Belizean vowel patterns.

8. The notation "zero-English morpheme" (e.g., /∅ Cop/) in no way implies that the actual English morpheme (/be/ in this case) is present at some underlying level of the creole system and then deleted; any occurrence of an English morpheme is best understood as an addition. The notation used merely constitutes a convenient label which denotes that a given function of the English system is unmarked in the creole system, or marked in other ways, even though it is marked in terms of the English system elsewhere along the continuum.

9. De-iterative morphemes are not incorporated in this study.

APPENDIX
Basic Informant Data (Placencia Creoles)

Sample No.	Sex/Age	Origin	Residence	Occupation
Errol (1,8,16)	M:26	Placencia	Placencia	accountant
Dudu (2)	M:23	Placencia	Placencia	fisherman
Toni (3)	M:25	Placencia	Belize-City	fisherman
Sonia (4,11)	F:45	Placencia	Placencia	housewife, Village Council member
Blink (5)	M:28	Placencia	Placencia	fisherman, barman
Philip (6)	M:29	Belize-City	Belize-City	artist
Andrew (7)	M:53	Belize-City	Placencia	night watchman
Doris (9)	F:64	Placencia	Placencia	postmistress, Village Council member
Lucille (10)	F:39	Placencia	Placencia	housewife
Karim (12)	M:23	Belize-City	Placencia	unemployed
Tensy (13)	F:43	Placencia	Placencia	housewife
Eddie (14)	M:28	Boom	Placencia	teacher
Peter (15)	M:40	Boom	Belize-City	government official
Flowers (17)	M:35	Monkey River	Placencia	priest, school principal

SOCIOLINGUISTIC HISTORY AND THE CREOLIST*

John Holm
College of the Bahamas

As it has grown clear that sociolinguistic perspectives offer new insights into an ever-broadening range of language problems, including language development and change in progress (e.g., Labov 1965), creolists find themselves in the fortunate position of studying language varieties that evolved comparatively recently in social contexts that are often surprisingly well documented. Since the pioneering work of LePage (LePage and DeCamp 1960), there has been an increasing appreciation of the important interrelationship between the development of a creolized language variety and the social history of its speakers. However, despite the many breakthroughs in quantitatively linking social and linguistic data in synchronic studies (Labov 1966; Trudgill 1974), the two have yet to be directly linked in a diachronic study.

This study suggests two possible approaches to linking social and linguistic data to gain insight into the history of a creole and its speakers. Both approaches deal with current lexical items in Nicaragua's Miskito Coast Creole (MCC),† items which in the source language represent both archaisms and regionalisms.

MCC represents one of the oldest varieties of English spoken outside Britain, having been brought to the Caribbean coast of Central America in the first half of the 17th century by British traders from the ill-fated Puritan colony on Providence Island (1630-41) and then by buccaneers. The latter found allies against the Spanish in the Miskito, an Afro-Indian people who adopted a pidginized form of English for contact while retaining their mother tongue, a Macro-Chibchan language. MCC had developed into a creole by the 1700s when the area became a British colony for some fifty years. In the 1780s the Spanish drove out the British settlers who retreated with their slaves to Belize and elsewhere, but some Creoles stayed on. Their language has survived two centuries of isolation from mainstream English, resisting until quite recently any notable influence from Spanish. MCC has developed along its own lines to meet the needs of its speakers in their particular circumstances. It has also become the first language of most of

* This study was supported by a grant from the University of London's Central Research Fund; it is with pleasure that I acknowledge this assistance.

† Data were collected in part during fieldwork in Bluefields, Nicaragua in 1976.

Nicaragua's Carib and Rama Indians, the latter having developed it into a distinct creole of their own (Rama Cay Creole).

For natural and cultural phenomena unknown in Britain, MCC has hundreds of words from African languages, Miskito, and Spanish. The main part of its lexicon, however, has evolved from English; many items are formally, semantically, or syntactically distinct from their English etyma, or occur in new combinations (Holm 1978). Still others, the topic of this study, are derived from words which today in Britain are considered archaic or regional.

Archaisms

Miskito Coast Creole contains words whose etyma seem to have disappeared from standard English usage as early as the 16th century, according to the latest usage with the current MCC meaning cited in the *Oxford English Dictionary*. Thus the dates of the latest *OED* citation (LOCs) span four centuries. To see if any correlation could be made between periods of greater borrowing and those periods of Miskito Coast history likely to have been characterized by intense contact between English and MCC, some one hundred MCC words now archaic in Britain were arranged chronologically by LOC dates, ranging from 1513 to 1886. However, on the advice of LePage, items with LOCs after the early 19th century were excluded since their obsolete nature was not always clear at the time the *OED* was compiled. The remaining items are presented in Table 1, MCC Archaisms Grouped Chronologically, on pp. 42-43. The three centuries from 1513 to 1814 were divided into fifty-year periods whose portions of the total are shown in graph form in Figure 1, MCC Archaisms and Miskito Coast History, p. 45. The percentage of archaisms from each half century, based on LOC dates, is given along with known dates of historical periods when intensive borrowing was likely to have occurred. There does indeed seem to be a correlation between the social and linguistic data that can be quantified.

This study represents a search for a method of procedure, and its exploratory nature must be borne in mind. Furthermore, some of the basic premises need to be carefully examined. It must be asked, for example, whether the implied relationship between the LOC date and the time of the actual borrowing into MCC might not, in fact, be an unwarranted assumption. Clearly the borrowing could have occurred either before or after the word dropped out of standard usage (or, more precisely, happened to be written down in a work that happened to survive until the *OED* was compiled). For the many items in Table 1 marked *D* (still current in certain British dialects at the end of the 19th century when the *English Dialect Dictionary* was compiled), there is no way to determine whether the word was borrowed at an earlier period when it was still current in standard usage, or later when it was obsolete in standard but possibly still current in regional

Table 1
MCC Archaisms Grouped Chronologically

1513	D	breed	be pregnant
1513		neither	no, nor
1526	D	corruption	pus
1535		law	custom
1540		niceness	fine food
1551		one	especially
1552		cratch	scratch
1561		quart	quarter
1571		god-brother	male peer
1575		ram goat	male goat
1597	A	sick	to be ill
1598		bride	bridegroom
1601	D	howsomever	however
1601	D	whatsomever	whatever
1602	D	from	since
1606		cry upon	complain
1606	D	whosomever	whoever
1606	D	dark	to get dark
1607		bring out	bear
1611		again	(no) longer
1613		mangrowe	mangrove
1622		sake of	because of
1629		consort	accomplice
1632	D	self	same, very
1633	D	high	to rise
1634	D	Chinee	a Chinese
1634		fisherman	kingfisher
1647	D	full	to fill
1648	D	smokey	foggy
1651	D	shame	to be awed
1656	D	prog	to beg
1658		moon calf	monster
1661	A	foot	foot, leg
1661		grudge	to envy
1669	D	remind	remember
1678		clammish	astringent

continued

Table 1 (continued):

1681		staff	harpoon shaft
1682		baby of eye	pupil
1691		night walker	kinkajou
1692		shuffle	move on belly
1694		foot-track	foot-print
1697		harpoon	knife on tip
1700	D	soon	early
1700	D	stinkard	stinker
1703		country	native
1703		gable-end	gable
1712		cloddy	sour (milk)
1725		all-heal	an herb
1725	D	bubby	breast
1726	S	molest	annoy
1729		hear	obey
1732		bore	push through a crowd
1733	D	ground	field
1743		night butterfly	moth
1750		crabbed	greedy, cruel
1751	A	hand	hand, arm
1755		out street	outskirts
1764		pockwood	lignum vitae
1781		cry	squeak (leather)
1781		wench	wanton woman
1782		couteau	small machete
1787	D	burying	funeral
1790		cocoa	cacao
1794		chocolate tree	cacao tree
1799		sick	sick person
1800		pruen	prune tree
1801		bounce	run into
1801		make up	make (a fire)
1801	D	why for	why
1805	S	support	endure
1808		all	even
1808		piece	field
1809	D	ram cat	male cat
1814	D	company	give companionship

usage. A further complication is the impossibility of determining whether parallel usage in Spanish (items marked *S*) or African (items marked *A*) languages represents an alternate or a convergent source of influence.

The most that can be surmised is that words such as *howsomever* (LOC 1601) are somewhat more likely to have been borrowed into MCC during the 17th rather than the 19th century. If this is the case, then Figure 1 can indicate general trends regarding periods of intensified lexical borrowing. If, on the other hand, the LOC date and the date of borrowing are unrelated, then the graph reveals very little.

Fortunately, some evidence supporting the existence of such a relationship can be found. Had MCC been a written language, one could simply go through the literature looking for earliest occurrences of words, then compare these with LOC dates. The next best resource would seem to be surviving documents written on the Miskito Coast by travelers and others. One such is *Mr. Penrose: The Journal of Penrose, Seaman,* the semi-fictional account of a Welshman stranded on the Miskito Coast, written in 1783 by William Williams, a Welshman who seems to have had close firsthand knowledge of this area. Judging from linguistic evidence (e.g., authentic names in Rama, the language of a very small and obscure tribe of Indians, as well as Williams' use of words which survive today on the Miskito Coast but nowhere else, to the best of my knowledge), it seems likely that Williams, like Penrose, had spent a considerable amount of time among the Rama, who then occupied an area to the south of Bluefields Lagoon. Since communication with the Indians took place in simplified English (in the book and almost certainly also in fact), Williams' English is interesting not only as a possible reflection of its use there at that time, but also because it (or something similar) must have been providing the models on which MCC English words were being based.

In this light, Williams' English illuminates the above problem of the correlation between LOC dates and the time of borrowing into MCC. In reference to a small field he had earlier cleared and cultivated, the narrator speaks of going back to "the Old Plantation where I visited my old *Grounds*" (p. 321). The last word is used in its current MCC sense of 'cultivated field' (count noun). Since the LOC date for this meaning of *ground* is 1733, Williams' use of this word provides at least one fairly straightforward case of the known use of a word on the Miskito Coast within a century (in this case, precisely fifty years) from the time this particular usage was last cited in Standard English. It would seem likely, then, that other archaisms became established in MCC within a comparable period.

Regionalisms

A Creole friend declared, only partly in jest, that anyone claiming membership in the Bluefields aristocracy should be prepared to produce in his genealogy at least one Miskito princess and one Scottish sea captain. There is indeed an oral

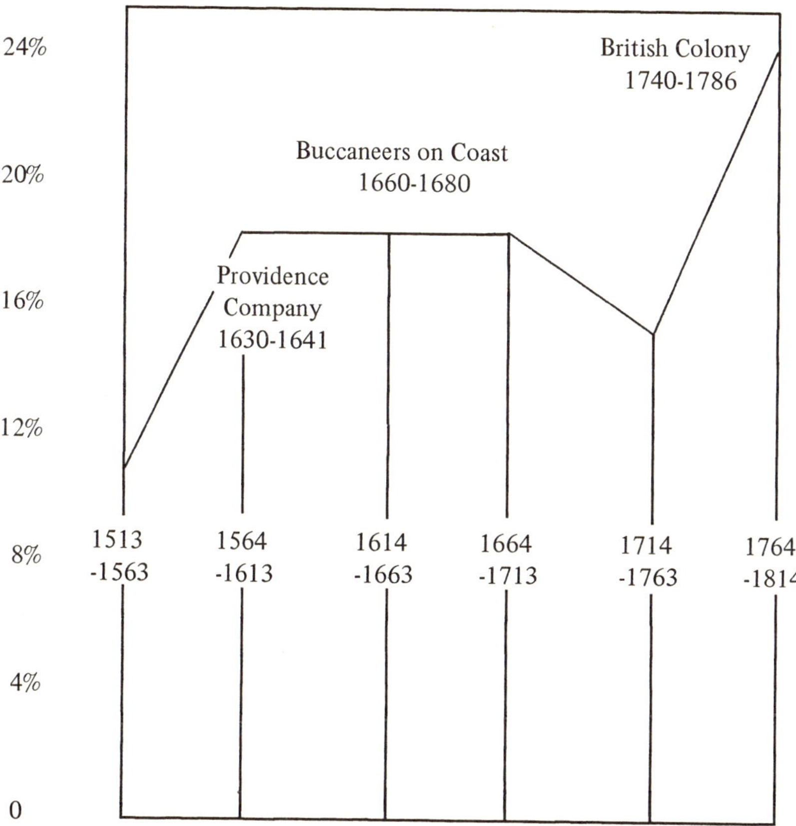

Figure 1
MCC Archaisms and Miskito Coast History

tradition among MCC speakers that their British ancestors were largely Scotsmen. Although there are scattered references in the literature on the area supporting this, such as Strangeway's (1822:13) remark that "the Mosquito Shore . . . has always been the darling object of the Scotch," there are no surviving records dealing with the local origin in Britain of those settlers who went to the 18th-century colony. This is not surprising in that most of these settlers, like their working-class contemporaries elsewhere, were illiterate and thus not in a position to leave such information behind. In this respect, almost as little is known about the local origin of the Creoles' ancestors from Europe as about those from Africa.

With a view to finding clues on this subject, British regionalisms borrowed into MCC were examined in the following manner. In Table 2, Regional British Dialect Usages Current in MCC, pp. 47-49, MCC terms with cognates in the *English Dialect Dictionary (EDD)* are listed with an indication of the region in Britain in which they were still found at the end of the last century. To tabulate a composite picture of which regions contributed most heavily to the Central American creole, a count was made of each column for region (i.e., G, 1, 2, 3, etc.) to see how many tokens it contained, and what portion this represented of the total number of tokens (rather than words—this being necessary to account for items found in more than one region). These sums and percentages, summarized in Table 3, p. 49, are the basis for Figure 2, The Provenance of British Regionalisms in Miskito Coast Creole, on p. 50.

It is interesting to what extent Figure 2 corroborates the Creoles' oral tradition of their ancestors' Scots and Northcountry origins: over 40 percent of all British regionalisms in their language come from these two areas. Yet how closely does Figure 2 represent actual migration patterns? Several complicating factors must be carefully examined before attempting to draw any conclusions. First, as discussed above, the double status of certain items (e.g., *bubby* 'breast', or *from* 'since') as both archaisms and regionalisms points up the impossibility of clearly separating the two categories. There is no way of knowing whether the conjunction *from,* for example, was introduced into MCC by Londoners when it was still current in the standard, or later on by Scots after it had become a regionalism.

Secondly, these figures are only as reliable as the works on which they are based, and there is indication that contributions to Wright's *English Dialect Dictionary* were spotty indeed; a few enthusiastic vicar-philologists in one area and the lack of them in another could make an item found throughout both regions appear to occur in only one. Loreto Todd, feeling that my original figures (based on the *EDD* alone) did not reflect the many Irish usages known to her (but not indicated in the *EDD*), revised my first version of Table 2 by adding tokens to the column for Ireland; this resulted in a doubling of the portion of the tokens for Ireland (15 percent vs. 7.5 percent).

Table 2
Regional British Dialect Usages Current in Miskito Coast Creole

Key: G General; 1 Ireland; 2 Wales; 3 Scotland; 4 Northcountry; 5 West Midlands; 6 East Midlands; 7 East Anglia; 8 Home Counties; 9 Westcountry

Usage	G	1	2	3	4	5	6	7	8	9
arm-hole 'armpit'		1			4	5	6		8	
at 'to'		1			4					
atween 'between'	G	1		3						
ax 'ask'	G	1		3						
baby (of eye) 'pupil'				3						
back 'carry on back'									8	
backways 'backwards'					4					
bawl 'shout, cry'		1			4				8	9
belly-work 'diarrhea'					4					
bank 'estate, farm'					4					
best 'had better'	G	1								
blow 'breathe; rest'				3	4					
booboo 'bogeyman'				3	4		6			
bro' 'male peer'								7		
brogues 'stout shoes'		1		3	4					
bruck 'break'		1		3						
bubby 'breast'				3						
buck 'butt'		1			4	5			8	
buck-mouth 'buck-teeth'		1		3	4					
bunky 'buttocks'										9
burying 'funeral'	G	1		3						
by 'by the time that'				3						
carry 'take, escort'		1			4					
clean 'clear off land'		1					6			
cloyed 'tired (of food)'					4		6			
coat 'petticoat'				3	4			7		9
cock-up-bubby 'plant sp.'									8	
company 'give companionship'				3						
cow 'bull, calf, cow'				3						
crabbid 'cruel, greedy'		1		3						
cranky 'unstable (boats)'					4		6		8	
crimpy 'thin, bent over'					4			7		
doctor fish 'fish species'				3						
doctor fly 'insect species'				3	4					
dodge 'follow stealthily'				3	4					
drudge 'dredge'		1								9
drugs 'dregs'										9
drownded 'drown'		1			4	5	6			
duff 'raisin cake'		1							8	9
evening 'afternoon'		1				5		7		
fall 'fell (timber)'		1							8	9
fass 'meddle, disturb'		1		3	4					
favor 'resemble'	G	1								
first 'immediately'					4	5				9
for 'to (+ verb)'		1			4					9
from 'since (conj.)'		1		3						
frowzy 'musty'	G	1		3						
full 'to fill'				3	4					
gal 'girl'	G							7	8	
galiwasp 'lizard species'	G				4					9
gaulin 'heron species'				3						
gibbridge 'gibberish'					4					
gig 'spinning top'	G	1		3						
go abroad 'go out'		1		3					8	9
grain 'unit (hair, peas)'		1		3	4				8	
grater 'to grate'					4					9
'gree 'agree; get along'					4			7		9
ground 'field'	G	1		3						
goddy 'godmother'				3	4					
hall 'livingroom'					4					9
hear 'understand'								7		
high 'to rise (of tide)'					4		6		8	
hoggish 'quick-tempered'							6			
hoss 'horse'					4		6	7	8	9
hot 'heat up (food)'	G									
holding 'embracing'				3						
hucks 'husk'									8	9
junk 'chunk'				3	4					9

continued

Table 2 (continued):

just now 'soon'	G	1								
kiver 'pot cover'	G	1		3						
learn 'teach'	G	1		3						
leff 'leave'		1								9
leg seed 'swollen gland'				3	4					
lick 'a blow'	G	1		3						
lickle 'little'						5				
light cake 'risen cake'					4	5		7		
liard 'liar'		1								9
long pig 'human flesh'	G	1								
look 'search for'		1				5				
loose 'to unfasten'		1		3						
loss 'to lose'		1		3	4					9
mager 'skinny'				3						
man 'term of address'				3						
mannish 'impudent'					4				8	
mash 'crush; destroy'					4		6			
matter 'to care about; heed'					4					9
middle-day 'noon'						5		7		9
middle-night 'midnight'				3						
mines 'mine (poss. pn.)'				3						
mug 'pitcher, jug'					4			7	8	
natural 'entirely, quite'										9
nose-hole 'nostril'					4		6		8	
old wife 'fish species'					4					9
onliest 'only'					4				8	9
osnabrig 'coarse cloth'				3						
out 'put out (a light)'									8	
out 'oust; eject'				3	4					
pan 'can (not shallow)'					4					
partner 'companion'					4					
pop 'to strike'				3					8	
pop 'a blow'				3					8	
poppy-show 'foolish(ness)'				3						
pick 'gather (shellfish)'		1				5	6			
pissabed 'plant species'	G	1		3						
présent 'give (a gift)'					4					
pure 'very; much; only'					4		6	7		9
pussly 'plant species'	G									
pyatka 'magpie'				3						
quail 'to wilt (plants)'										9
rank 'bad-smelling'					4					
reach 'arrive (absolute)'				3	4	5				
rhyme 'a joke; anecdote'		1	2							
rump-hole 'anus'				3						
run-down 'stew'										9
run sea 'surf with canoe'								7		
score 'slash someone with a razor'				3						
search 'look through (a book)'		1				5				
set-up 'a wake'				3	4					
shadow 'reflection; ghost'		1			4					
shoove 'shove'				3	4	5	6			
slide 'to edge; sneak'				3						
smallen 'make smaller'	G									
squis(h) 'squeeze; squash'				3					8	9
stay 'reside'					4					
stick-leg 'wooden leg'		1		3						
stick-to-me-ribs 'pastry'					4					
stuff '(obeah) medicine'					4			7	8	
study 'steady'										9
study 'ponder; grieve'					4					9
swinge 'singe'	G	1								
teeth 'tooth'				3						
titty 'sister'				3	4					
them 'they'					4		6		8	
them 'those'	G									
them-here 'these'	G									
them-there 'those'					4	5	6			
to 'at'			2	3		5	6			9
today day 'nowadays'										9
trust 'lend (money)'				3	4				8	9
turn 'turn into; become'				3						
watergall 'rainbow'	G									

continued

Table 2 (continued):

walk 'excursion, trip'										9
whe 'that; which; who'					4					
winjy 'scrawny'								7		
worser 'worse'	G	1								
worserer 'worse'	G									
worsest 'worst'	G									
yalla 'yellow'		1			4				8	9
wrothèd 'very angry'									8	
yerry 'hear; understand'					4					9
yeye 'eye'										9

Table 3
Sums and Percentages of Regional British Dialect Usages Current in Miskito Coast Creole

	Region	Tokens	Percent of Total
G	General	23	7.5
1	Ireland	46	15.0
2	Wales	2	0.5
3	Scotland	64	21.0
4	Northcountry	62	20.0
5	West Midlands	15	5.0
6	East Midlands	18	6.0
7	East Anglia	14	5.0
8	Home Counties	25	8.0
9	Westcountry	38	12.0
	totals	307	100.0

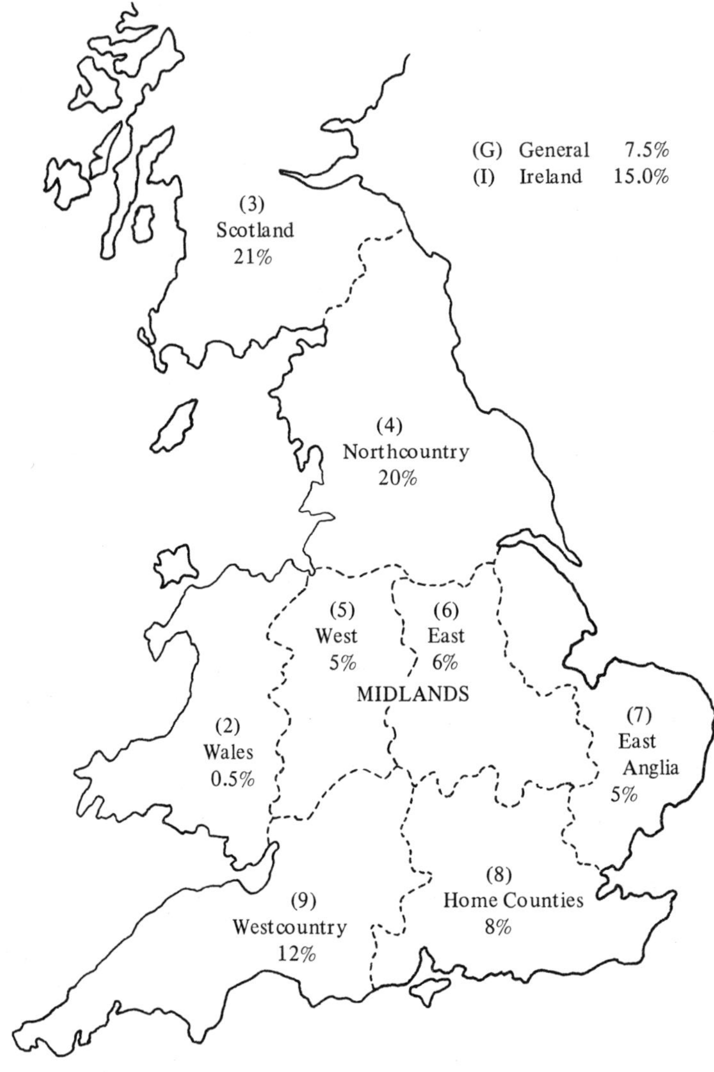

Figure 2
The Provenance of British Regionalisms in Miskito Coast Creole

A third factor to consider is that outlying areas (e.g., Scotland, Ireland, and the Northcountry) may in part appear to have contributed a higher proportion of regionalisms to MCC simply because of the greater likelihood of archaisms being retained longer farther from the standard language's political, economic, and cultural center of gravity in London. A fourth consideration is both the relative and absolute population figures for each region. Thus Wales, very thinly populated until the advent of large-scale coal mining in the last century, appears to have contributed fewer regionalisms to MCC than any other area. Or does this again reflect the biases of the *EDD?*

Finally, it is by no means certain where this particular brew of regionalisms was distilled: on the Miskito Coast? in Jamaica? at sea? in the baracoons of West Africa? It is likely that the English (pidgin, creole, or unsimplified) spoken in all these places played some role in determining the lexical composition of what became MCC. Thus MCC *buck* 'butt', while undoubtedly coming originally from the Northcountry, may have come via Jamaica and reflect migration to the latter rather than to the Miskito Coast. Indeed, Jamaican *bok* may derive from Sranan *buku* 'butt', brought to the island by displaced British settlers and slaves from Surinam in the 1670s (Cassidy 1961:12), while *buku* may well have come to Surinam from West Africa, rather than directly from the Northcountry.

The provenance of British regionalisms in Sierra Leone's Krio (Hancock 1971: 125) and in Bahamian English (my own current research) is strikingly similar to the picture presented for MCC in Figure 2: in the main, the relative ordering of the regions is the same. Although the proportional contributions of the various regions to the general pool of British laborers going to the colonies might be reflected in this similarity, it nonetheless seems unlikely that each colony represented that general mixture in miniature. Had there been no pattern of emigration to those colonies where there were already kinsmen or former neighbors who could make the move easier, it is doubtful that there could have arisen any colonial societies characterized by their regional origin in Britain, supposedly the case of such "essentially Scotch" communities as Belize (Forbes 1911:171). Similarities in lexicon, like those in syntax, seem rather to point to the diffusion of forms occasioned by the mobility of language-carriers in these maritime colonies.

Yet in conclusion, despite all the above caveats and cautions, Figure 2 would still seem to cast considerable light on regional British migration patterns to the Miskito Coast, if only because there has been nearly total darkness on this subject to date. In proceeding with the more formidable task of searching for lexical clues to migration patterns from Africa, similar sources of possible distortion and complication should be borne in mind.

HALFWAY BETWEEN QUECHUA AND SPANISH: The Case for Relexification[1]

Pieter Muysken
University of Amsterdam

1. Introduction

Media Lengua (ML hereafter) is a fascinating Amerindian contact language spoken in several communities in the Ecuadorian Highlands. It is Quechua in its grammatical structure, and almost 90 percent Spanish in its lexicon (see Table 1, p. 53). It has been in existence for over 60 years, and it has native speakers as well as speakers for whom it is the second or third language with Quechua and/or Spanish.

The aims of this paper are threefold: 1) to describe a case of massive relexification, resulting from the contact of two typologically, extremely different languages; 2) to present a linguistic theory of relexification, and to analyze the change and variation in the grammar of Quechua which are the consequences of its relexification by Spanish; and 3) to analyze the role of relexification in a general theory of language genesis, in trying to explain why Quechua was relexified at all.

2. Media Lengua

The recent bibliography of pidgins and creole languages by Reinecke et al. (1975) devotes only four pages to those South American regions where Spanish has been in intensive contact with indigenous languages for centuries, and but a handful of items to contact languages there. Likewise, Lavandera's (1974) review article about sociolinguistic work done on New World Spanish deals mostly with studies made in Argentina, the United States, Mexico, and Panama, and only briefly with Paraguay and the Andean area.

Considering the paucity of materials relating to the contact between Spanish and the indigenous languages (a striking exception is Albò's *Social Constraints on Cochabamba Quechua,* 1970), one is led to believe that no phenomena of interest to the student of pidgins and creoles are to be discovered here. This expectation is in accordance with Diebold's (1961:109) prediction that no pidgins could emerge out of the contact situation of Indian languages and Spanish in Mexico since the sociological circumstances did not favor their emergence. No sudden need for communication between speakers of different languages, which would lead to a makeshift language, is present (cf. Whinnom 1971).

The fact is that we do indeed find very interesting contact phenomena involving

Quechua, an Indian language of the Andean region, and Spanish. The contact language studied here, Media Lengua, is not used for communication among different ethnic groups, but only within the community itself. In the final section of this paper we will try to explain why it emerged at all, but the fact that it is an intra-group, and not an inter-group, language accounts for some of its characteristics such as its conservative Quechua grammar and phonology.

Although several other varieties have been studied, the ML described here is spoken around the town of San Miguel de Salcedo, in the Cotopaxi province of Ecuador, by Indian peasants, weavers, and construction workers.[2] The area, situated at an altitude of 2.800 meters, is one of the poorest in a poor country; but it is relatively accessible from the capital, Quito. Fieldwork on Quechua (Q), rural Spanish (Sp), and ML in the area was carried out in the period 1974-76 and in 1978 (cf. Muysken 1977; Stark & Muysken 1977; Muysken 1979). Three samples of ML were gathered, totaling about four hours of conversation of five speakers. Sample CF represents data elicited from a 30-year-old couple, both native speakers; sample CI represents conversational data from these same speakers and their children, recorded two years later; sample MI represents conversational data of a female 37-year-old native speaker of ML, and two nonnative speakers of ML. Sample CF clearly represents a conservative norm for ML, while samples CI and MI show cases of ML-Sp code-switching, as well as innovations within ML, as will be argued in Section 3 of this paper. Still, the three samples show a remarkable degree of uniformity in essential respects, such as the amount of Spanish vocabulary present (see Table 1 below).

Table 1
The Etymological Origin of the Verbal Roots in the Three Samples

	CF	CI	MI	Total	%
not a verb in Sp	6	11	8	25	1%
Q verb	41 (20)*	91 (57)*	63 (31)*	195 (108)*	11% (6%)*
Sp verb	309	849	414	1572	87%
indeterminate		3	3	6	
% Sp verbs	87%	89%	85%	87%	

*the number in parentheses indicates occurrences of the Q verb /ga-/ 'to be'

What is ML? Basically, it is Q with a lexicon almost completely derived from Sp, but which to a large extent preserves the semantic and syntactic structures of Q. An example is given in /1/:

/1/ Q yalli-da tamia-pi-ga, mana ri-sha-chu[3]
ML dimas-ta llubi-pi-ga, no i-sha-chu
too-much rain-SUB-TO, not go-1FU-NEG[4]
Sp si llueve demás, no voy a ir
'if it rains too much, I won't go'

Here we see that ML preserves the Q grammar almost completely: SOV word order, the use of verbal affixes (here the adverbial subordinator /-pi/) to indicate subordination, topic and negation marking (/-ga/ and /-chu/, respectively), person and tense affixation rather than inflection of a paradigm.

Sp irregular verbs are regularized in ML. As shown in the following chart, they derive from inflected or infinitve Sp forms:

/2/ ML	Sp	
i-	ir	'go'
(bamuchi	vámonos	'let's go')
da-/dali-	dar (dale)	'give'
bi-	ver	'see'
azi-	hacer	'do'
ri-	reíse	'laugh'
dintra-	entrar/dentrar	'enter'
sabi-	saber	'know'

These verbs receive the normal Q affixes:

/3/ ML no *sabi*-ni-chu
Q mana yacha-ni-chu
Sp no sé
'I don't know'

/4/ ML ya *i*-gri-ni
Q ña ri-gri-ni
Sp ya me voy
'I'm already going'

/5/ ML bos-mu *da*-ni-mi
Q kan-mu ku-ni-mi
Sp te doy a tí
'I give to you'

Besides verb regularization we find several other processes of lexical adaptation of Sp vocabulary in ML, such as "freezing," reduplication, and morphological regularization to fit the Q CVCV pattern:

/6/ "Freezing": the combination in the ML lexicon of morphologically separate Sp forms:

Sp	ML	
no ha habido	nuwabishka nuwábi	'there has been no . . .'
no hay	núway	'there is no . . .'
aún no	aúnu	'not yet'
a mí	ami	'me' (non-nominative pron.)

/7/ Reduplication
ML yo-ga *bin-bin* tixi-y-da pudi-ni
Sp yo puedo tejer muy bien
'I can weave very well'
ML anda-y *brebe-brebe* kuzina-ngi
Sp anda a cocinar breve
'go cook quickly'

/8/ Morphological Regularization
Sp relój
ML relóxo
Q rílux
'watch'

By far the most interesting process of adaptation of the Sp lexicon in ML has been relexification. Relexification, which will be more technically defined in the next section of this paper, can be described as the process of vocabulary borrowing in which the borrowed element adopts the meaning and use of the element in the receptor language for which it is substituted. Examples in ML are /sinta-/ and /sinta-ri-/:

/9/ Q tiya-
ML sinta-
Sp estar sentado, vivir, estar, hay
'sit', 'live', '(loc. be)', 'there is'

Q tiya-ri-
ML sinta-ri-
SP sentarse
'sit down'

In these cases, a single ML word is substituted for the Q word, preserving the various meanings of the latter even when in Sp each of these meanings may be expressed by a separate lexical item. Here the claim is made that relexification is in fact the general process responsible for the formation of the ML lexicon.

A very interesting and complicated case involves the ML verbs /kiri-/ 'wish' and /dizi- ∿ zi-/ 'want', 'say'. In Q two verbs exist which express wishing and wanting:

/10/ Q muna- 'wish'
ni- 'want', 'say'

These verbs occur in constructions such as:

/11a/ Q	papa-da muna-ni potatoAC wish-1sg	'I want potatoes'
/11b/	papa-da ni-ni potatoAC want-1sg	'I want potatoes'
/11c/	miku-na muna-ni eat-NOM wish-1sg	'I want to eat'
/11d/	miku-sha ni-ni eat-1FU say-1sg	'I say I'll eat', 'I want to eat'

In Q both verbs, /ni-/ and /muna-/, can take NP complements and infinitival complements. In the latter case, /ni-/ selects /-sha/ on the infinitive verb, and /muna-/ selects /-na/ or another marker.

In ML we find that: a) Q /muna-/ has been relexified as ML /kiri-/ 'want' (Sp 'querer'), and Q /ni-/ has been relexified as ML /(di)zi-/ 'wish', 'say' (Sp 'decir'); b) with NP complements only ML /kiri-/ occurs; and c) with infinitival complements /kiri-/ often gets /-na/ or another nominalizer, and /(di)zi-/ often, but not always gets /sha/ complements.

We notice that the relexification process has been only partial here. Whereas in Q the verb /ni-/ can take NP complements, the corresponding ML item /(di)zi-/ cannot. We will return to the alternation between /dizi-/ and /zi/ in the next section of this paper.

Table 2
The Complements of /kiri-/ and /(di)zi-/ 'want' in the Three Samples

	kiri-			dizi-		
	CF	CI	MI	CF	CK	MI
NP-da	2		1			
NP-∅	1		1			
V-sha	1	2		4	2	1
V-na	3	1				1
V-na-da		1				
V-nga-bu		1				
V-y		1				

A second complex case of relexification involves the ML pronoun system. Consider the paradigm of personal pronouns in the three languages:

/12/ Q	ML	Sp	
ñuka	yo/ami+case	yo/me/mí	'I'
kan	bos	tu/te/tí	'you (intimate)'
		vos/te	'you (familiar)'
		usted/le	'you (polite)'
pay	el	él/le	'he'
		ella/le	'she'
ñukunchi	nustru	nosotros/nos	'we'
kan-guna	bos-kun	ustedes/les	'you (pl.)'
pay-guna	el-kuna	ellos/les	'they (m.)'
		ellas/les	'they (f.)'

The third column for this paradigm includes for Sp not only the nominative form but also the object clitic form and the non-nominative form where this differs from the nominative.

When we compare the three paradigms, we notice that the ML and the Q systems are very similar, and that /bos-kuna/ 'you (pl.)' is a direct relexification of Q /kan-guna/. Similarly, ML /el-kuna/ and Q /pay-guna/. The cases of ML /bos/ and /el/ are a little more complicated since both relexification and target simplification could be involved here; distinctions existing in Sp are lost. The only direct counter-example to relexification is the non-nominative personal pronoun ML /ami/, which was discussed already in /6/ as a case of freezing. This pronoun occurs with the Q case markers /-da/ 'acc.' and /-mu/ 'dat.' as in /13/:

/13/ ML ami-mu da-ngi
Q ñuka-mu ku-ngi
Sp le darás a mí
'give it to me'

In Table 3, all pronouns in the samples are listed, showing some deviations from the ML paradigm given in /12/. These will be discussed in the next section.

Table 3
Personal Pronouns in the Three Samples

		CF	CI	MI	Total
I	yo	31	24	28	83
	ami+case	10	3	1	12
	ami (obj.)		1		1
	me (obj.)	1			1
	miu (subj.)			1	1
II	bos	11	2	6	19
	bos-kuna	1	2	1	4
	tu	1			1
III	el	7	13	10	20
	el-kuna	3	10	7	20
	ele		1		1
1pl.	nustru	3	19	13	35
	nustrus		1	1	2
	nosotros		1	1	2
	ñukuchi			1	1

A final complex case of relexification to be discussed in this section involves derived verbs in Q. An important difference between the Q and the Sp lexicon is that in Q modal suffixes are present (which are combined with the relatively few Q verbal roots to form a complex system of verbal expressions) whereas in Sp every action is expressed through a separate verbal root. The semantic differentiation possible in the two systems is comparable.

The Q root /riku-/ 'see' offers an example of this difference in /14/; many other examples similar to that of /riku-/ could be given:

/14/		∅	ver	'see'
	riku-	ri	asomar, parecer, se ve	'appear'
		chi	mostrar, hacer ver	'show'
		ra	espiar, mirar fijamente	'stare'

In ML we find three processes operant in the formation of complex verbal expressions: a) straightforward adoption of the Sp lexical item; b) adoption of the Sp root corresponding with the Q root, combined with the Q derivational suffixes; and c) adoption of an Sp root not corresponding to a Q root, combined with a Q derivational suffix. The combination of these three possibilities gives us the paradigm in /15/ which corresponds to /14/, and which is illustrated in Table 4:

/15/ Q		ML	Sp	
riku-	(a)	bi-	ver	'see'
	(a)	mustra-	mostrar	'show'
riku-chi-	(b)	bi-chi-	hacer ver	'make see'
	(c)	mustra-chi-	mostrar	'show'
	(a)	parisi-	parecer	'appear'
riku-ri-	(a)	asoma-	asomar	'show up'
	(b)	bi-ri-n	se ve	'it is seen'
	(a)	chapa-	chapar	'spy'
riku-ra-	(b)	bi-ra-	mirar fijamente	'stare'
	(c)	chapa-ra-	chapar	'spy'

When the Q has its literal meaning, often process (b) applies; when it has a derived meaning, (a) or (c) applies.

Table 4
The Verb 'to see' and Related Forms in the Three Samples

	CF	CI	MI	Total
bi-	10	1	1	12
be (imp.)		3		3
ber (inf.)		1		1
bes (2sg)			1	1

continued

Table 4 (continued):

	CF	CI	MI	Total
bi-ri-	1			1
asoma-	2			2
parisi-	1			1
bi-ra-	1			1
chapa-	1			1
chapa-ra-			1	1
bi-chi-	1			1
mustra-	1			1
mustra-chi-		2		2

In this section we have given a general description of ML; we have described some processes of vocabulary adaptation; and, in particular, we have presented some cases of relexification, showing its complexities. In the following section we will attempt a more technical definition of relexification as a specific type of vocabulary substitution; we will see in which ways relexification is constrained, how ML differs from Q syntactically, and along which dimensions we find variation in ML.

3. Relexification and Its Consequences

The previous section, describing different aspects of ML vocabulary, has already shown that one of the most interesting aspects of ML is the structure of its lexicon. If we accept the superficial definition of ML as a form of Q with Sp vocabulary, then ML must be seen as a compromise between the Q lexical system and the Sp one. We have already seen several instances of this compromise. Here the processes operating in it and the consequences it has for the grammar of the language will be studied more systematically. Specifically, the following questions will be discussed:

1) How can relexification and other types of vocabulary substitution be defined?
2) What linguistic constraints operate on vocabulary substitution?
3) In which way does the grammar of ML differ from that of Q, as a result of relexification?
4) Along which dimensions do we find variation in ML?

In order to give a technical definition of relexification, it is helpful to discuss the concept of lexical entry, as it has been defined in generative grammar. Jackendoff (1975) discusses this in detail. The lexicon of a language consists of an unordered series of lexical entries, which are essentially bundles of various types of information. An example is the lexical entry for the English verb 'decide', part of which is:

/16/

$$\begin{bmatrix} \text{/decid/} \\ +\text{V} \\ +\text{NP}_1 \;\_\_\; \text{on NP}_2 \\ \text{NP}_1 \text{ DECIDE ON NP}_2 \\ \text{NP}_1 = +\text{human} \end{bmatrix} \quad \begin{array}{l} \text{phonological representation} \\ \text{syntactic features} \\ \text{subcategorization features} \\ \text{semantic representation} \\ \text{selectional features} \end{array}$$

Here the phonological representation /decid/ is coupled with: 1) various syntactic features (specifying, among other things, that we are dealing with a verb); 2) subcategorization features (specifying that one of the complements of 'decide' is 'on NP'); 3) a semantic representation (left unspecified here but given in capitals); and 4) selectional features (indicating that the subject of 'decide' must be human, or at least animate).

Given the concept of lexical entry, relexification can be defined as the process of vocabulary substitution in which the only information adopted from the target language in the lexical entry is the phonological representation. This definition gives us the opportunity to define *translexification* as the process of vocabulary substitution in which, in addition to the phonological representation, all other levels of information are adopted from the target language as well. Schematically, these two options are given in /17/:

/17/ Vocabulary Substitution:

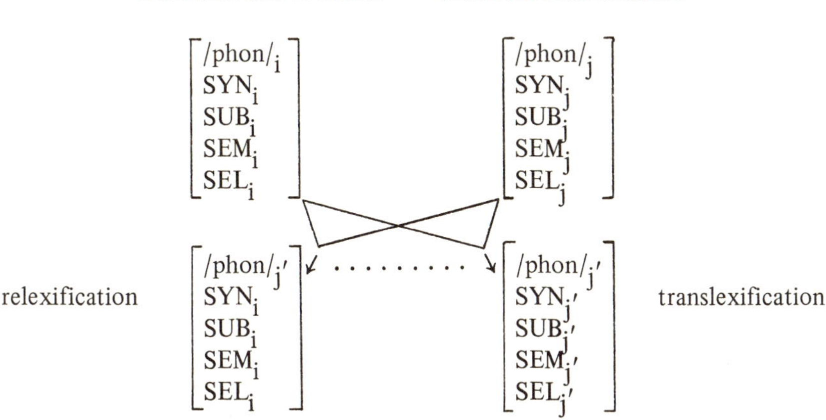

There are, of course, a number of outcomes intermediate between relexification and translexification, in which only some of the features of the target language item are adopted. Later in this section, we will see that the continuum between strict relexification and strict translexification is one of the parameters along which variation occurs in ML.

For relexification to occur, the semantic representations of source and target language entries must partially overlap; otherwise, the two entries would never be associated with each other. Other features of the two entries may, but need not, overlap. In ML, we find cases of relexification in which only part of the semantic representation of the two entries in Q and Sp overlaps, as in /18/, where the combination of the SP word *hambre* 'hunger' and the Q impersonal verb with animate object /yarika-(na)-/ 'to be hungry' has led to the ML impersonal verb /ambri-na-/:

/18/

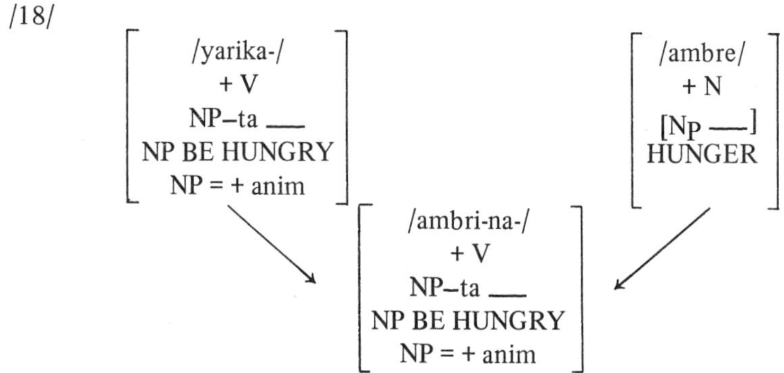

We have argued in the previous section that the major process operative in the creation of ML vocabulary was relexification. Consequently, we expect only those lexical categories to occur in ML that occur in Q. A survey of the different categories present in Q, Sp, and ML is given in /19/:

/19/	Sp	Q	ML	
	N	N	N	MAJOR
	V	V	V	
	A	A	A	
	P	–?	(P)	
	CONJUNCTION	–CONJ	CONJ, –CONJ	MINOR
	COMPLEMENTIZER	–	–	
	CLITIC PRONOUN	–	–	
	WH-PRONOUN	WH-PRO	WH-PRO	
	DEICTIC PRONOUN	DEI PRO	DEI PRO	

The expectation that the categories present in ML correspond to the categories in Q is largely borne out (as seen in /19/); however, there are several exceptions.

As shown in Table 5, several prepositions occur in the two samples CI and MI, but only /entre/ occurs in the formally elicited sample, CF.

Table 5
Prepositions in the Three Samples

	CF	CI	MI	Total
de		11	1	12
a		8	4	12
por		2	4	6
para		3	3	6
entre	2	2		4
komo			3	3
hasta		2	1	3
sin		1	2	3
en		2		2
despwesitu		1		1

The instances of /entre/ in ML could be regarded as relexification of the Q post-nominal element /-pura/, as in /20/:

/20/ ML entre seys-mi ga-nchi
Q sukta-pura-mi ga-nchi
six-among-AF be-1pl
Sp somos seis
'there are six of us'

In some ways, Q /-pura/ is distinct from the postpositions which mark case in Q and which can best be analyzed as case markers, not as elements of the category P. One of the rare instances of a true postposition (P) in Q may be /-pura/; hence, relexification as /entre/ would be expected. All other cases of Sp prepositions, with the exception of /despwesitu/ 'after', which occurs as an ML post-position (example /21/), will have to be considered as cases of code-switching in exclamations such as /pór dyos/ 'please'. Another instance of direct relexification is /21/:

/21/ML miza despwesitu kaza-mu i-naku-ndu-ga, ahí-bi buda da-naku-n
Q miza k'ipa wasi-mu ri-naku-pi-ga, chi-bi buda ku-naku-n
Mass after house-to go-PL-SUB-TO there feast give-PL-3
Sp yendo a la casa después de la Misa, ahí dan una boda
'going home after Mass, they then give a feast there'

Here /k'ipa/ may, again, be one of the few postpositions in Q. The alternative to treating the other cases of Sp prepositions as cases of code-switching is to assume that in ML we find two systems: the Sp prepositional system in a few cases, and the Q case marking system in the vast majority of cases.

An example of the introduction of an Sp preposition through code-switching as analyzed here is given in /22/:

/22/ sikyera karga-bu-lla-ish, pero *komi-nga-bu*-lla-ish da-chun, sikyera *para komir*
perhaps load-BEN-DIM-IND, but eat-NOM-BEN-DIM-IND give-SUB, perhaps for eat
'let them then give the food for a load, to eat, perhaps to eat'

Here /komi-nga-bu/, which contains the Q nominalizer /-nga-/ and the Q case marker /-bu-/, is juxtaposed to /para komir/, which contains the Sp preposition *para* and the Sp infinitive marker /-r/.

The case of conjunctions is complex. ML has adopted both the Sp and the Q system of conjunctions (see Table 6). In Q, conjunctions are always cliticized to the element on their left; but they are arguably generated as a separate phrase structure category (unlike case markers). In Sp we find conjunctions as a separate lexical category.

Table 6
Conjunctions in the Three Samples

	CF	CI	MI	Total
i	1	8	8	17
o	1	4	1	6
pero		11	2	13
sino ke		1		1
TOTAL	2	24	11	37

Are the Sp conjunctions that we find in ML cases of relexification of Q categories, or cases of introduction from Sp? The latter seems correct because: 1) in ML the conjunctions are used as in Sp; 2) the conjunctions coexist with the Q cliticized conjunctions; and 3) in Q itself we find frequent borrowing of Sp conjunctions. Only two Sp conjunctions are found in the CF sample, the probable reason being that only relatively short sentences were elictited.

Thus, the introduction of Sp conjunctions into ML is the one exception to the idea that ML lexical categories, arising through relexification, correspond strictly to Q categories. This exception may be explained by the fact that conjunctions, which occur at discourse level, are less closely integrated into the grammar of the language and can be borrowed more easily. The category of complementizers, for instance, is a much more crucial part of sentence grammar. We will turn to it in the following discussion.

To summarize our treatment of relexification, we can draw the following conclusions from the case of ML:

1) The different components of a lexical entry function so independently of each other that (apparently) a phonological representation can be substituted into an entry without affecting the other sets of features (syntactic, subcategorization, semantic, selectional).
2) For relexification to occur, the only requirement is that source and target language lexical entries share some semantic features; other common features are not required, although they will often be present.
3) A language which emerged through relexification has the same lexical categories as its source. The morphosyntactic and syntactic categories, which are expressed in Q through affixation, have been maintained in ML.

What consequences did relexification have for the syntax of ML? In which ways does it diverge from that of Q? Remarkably, relexification had relatively few consequences, for example: word order; comparatives; reflexives; embedded wh-questions and complementizers:

Word Order

In some cases the subcategorization features of the relexified item were adopted from Sp as well, which led to word order changes in ML. In /23/ we see an example involving the Sp preposition /entre/, which has already been discussed; in /24/, the example shows how a prenominal adjective in Q is relexified as a postnominal adjective in ML:

/23/ $\begin{bmatrix} +\mathrm{P} \\ \mathrm{N}\,\_\_ \end{bmatrix} \rightarrow \begin{bmatrix} +\mathrm{P} \\ \_\_\,\mathrm{N} \end{bmatrix}$

sukta-pura-mi	→	entre seys-mi
six-among-AF		among six-AF

/24/ $\begin{bmatrix} +\mathrm{A} \\ \_\_\,\mathrm{N} \end{bmatrix} \rightarrow \begin{bmatrix} +\mathrm{A} \\ \mathrm{N}\,\_\_ \end{bmatrix}$

k'uilla warmi	→	muhir bonita
pretty woman		woman pretty

On the whole, ML has maintained the SOV characteristics of Q, as can be seen in Table 7. Only 21 percent of the sentences in the three samples which contain both a verb and a complement in the VP (object, adverbial complement) show VX word order:

Table 7
VX vs. XV Word Order in the Three Samples

	CF	CI	MI	Total
VX	35	43	34	113
XV	160	132	125	417
VX/(VX+XV)	.18	.24	.22	.21
Not applicable	111	65	49	225
TOTAL	306	240	209	755

Comparatives

In Q, comparatives are formed with the uninflected verb /yalli/ 'surpass', which functions as a serial verb. The object with which something is compared receives /-da/ accusative case:

/25/Q kan Huzi-da *yalli* puri-ngi
you José-AC pass walk-2sg
'you walk faster than José'

In ML /yalli/ is relexified as /gana-/ 'win', but it cannot appear uninflected:

/26/ ML *bos Huzi-da *gana* anda-ngi
you José-AC win walk-2sg

Instead, /gana-/ must appear either in adverbial subordination with the /-sha/ marker, or in a coordinated clause:

/27/ ML Xwan-mi Pedro-da gana-sha grande ga-n
John-AF Peter-AC win-SUB big be-3
'John is taller than Peter'

/28/ Takunga-mi riko ga-n Salsedo-da gana-n
Latac.-AF rich be-3 Salcedo-AC win-3
'Latacunga is richer than Salcedo'

The impossibility of using uninflected /gana-/ in ML comparatives suggests that in some cases relexification can involve the simplification of a lexical entry. In Q /yalli/ must be marked to indicate its occurrence in serial VP contexts as well as in S contexts. Only the latter context, which allows for person marking, is preserved in ML, i.e., the context available to all verbs in the language.

Reflexives

Reflexives in Q do not involve a reflexive pronoun as they do in Sp. Instead, /-lladi/ 'just, precisely' is added to the subject NP:

/29/ Q ñuka-lladi riku-ni
I-just see-1sg
'I see myself'

With the 3rd person, /-lladi/ is added to the adverb /shina/ 'thus':

/30/ Q pay shina-lladi riku-n
he thus-just see-3
'he sees himself'

In ML, 3rd person reflexives are formed as in Q, with /shina/ being relexified as /asi/ 'thus' (from Sp *así*), but 1st person reflexives involve a double pronoun construction:

/31/ ML Huzi asi-lladi-mi mata-ka
José thus-just-AF kill-PA
'José killed himself'

/32/ ML *yo*-lladi bi-xu-ni *ami*-lla-da-di
I-just see-PR-1sg me-just-AC
'I see myself'

This construction is limited to the 1st person since, as seen in /12/, only that person has a separate non-nominative pronoun, /ami/.

While the resulting ML double pronoun construction could of course be interpreted as an adaptation to Sp syntax, this is by no means the necessary conclusion. In Sp the reflexive pronoun is an unstressed clitic in preverbal position. The ML reflexive element is a strong form which also occurs in nonreflexive contexts, as in /13/. Of course we do find stressed postverbal pronouns in Sp emphatic reflexives:

/33/ Sp yo me veo *a mî*
'I see mysélf'

In any case, the difference between Q and ML is specifically determined by a lexical element, /ami/, present in ML, absent in its source language.

Embedded Wh-Questions and Complementizers

In Q, embedded wh-questions are formed by fronting a wh-pronoun, as are non-embedded ones; but in addition they are nominalized, as are other embedded clauses. Compare /34a/ with /34b/ and /35a/ with /35b/:

/34a/ Q mana yacha-ni-chu [Xwan shamu-*shka*-da]
not know-1sg-NEG [John come-NOM-AC]
'I don't know that John has come'
/34b/ mana yacha-ni-chu [pi shamu-*shka*-da]
not know-1sg-NEG [who come-NOM-AC]
'I don't know who has come'
/35a/ mana yacha-ni-chu [Xwan shamu-*na*-da]
not know-1sg-NEG [John come-NOM-AC]
'I don't know that John will come'
/35b/ mana yacha-ni-chu [pi shamu-*na*-da]
not know-1sg-NEG [who come-NOM-AC]
'I don't know who will come'

Whereas the italicized nominalizers in /34/ and /35/ are part of the verb morphology, they are generally assumed to function as complementizers and are subcategorized by the matrix verb. The wh-pronoun /pi/ 'who', in /34b/ and /35b/, is fronted, but does not appear as the complementizer.

In ML, the situation is different. We find the /-na-/ and /-shka-/ nominalizers in sentential complements; but in embedded wh-questions we find ordinary verb inflection:

/36a/ ML no sabi-ni-chu [Xwan bini-*shka*-da]
not know-1sg-NEG [John come-NOM-AC]
/36b/ no sabi-ni-chu [kin bini-*rka*]
not know-1sg-NEG [who come-PA]
/36c/ *no sabi-ni-chu [kin bini-*shka*-da]
not know-1sg-NEG [who come-NOM-AC]

The contrast between /36/ and /34/ (a similar situation holds for /35/) suggests that in ML (where in embedded wh-questions the ordinary past tense marker /-rka-/ occurs instead of the nominalizer /-shka-/), the wh-element does function as the complementizer.

It would be tempting to interpret this development as the beginning of a typological shift from a COMP-final system (like Q) to a COMP-initial one (like Sp). The problem is that no or few other cases of clause-initial complementizers occur in ML. In Table 8 the data are given for /ki/ 'that', /porke/ 'because', and /aunke/ 'although':

Table 8
The Complementizer /ki/ in the Three Samples

	CF	CI	MI	Total
ki		5	1	6
porke		3		3
aunke	1	2		3

The three cases are somewhat different and will be analyzed separately. The 'that' complementizer /ki/ occurs as an alternative to /-shka-/ and /-na-/ complementation. Consider /37/:

/37/ no be *ki* no i-sha-chu dizi-*n*
not see that not go-1FU-NEG say-3
no ve que dice que no irá
'don't you see he does not want to go?'

no-mi kontra-*shka*-da abiza-ngi-chu
not AF find NOM AC tell 2sg NEG
no avisas que lo has encontrado
'don't tell that you found it'

Here /ki/ is part of the fixed expression /no be ki/, directly borrowed from Sp. Note that /be/ 'you see' does not receive Q person marking, whereas /dizi-n/, the verb in the domain of /ki/, receives main clause person marking. The next utterance (/38/) contains an example of a nominalized /-shka-/ complement:

/38/ pega-*shka* dizi-n dizi-ndo *ki* bos-kuna-ga *ke,* bos-kuna-lla-cha komi-*ngichi*
hit-NOM say-3 say-SUB that you-PL-TO that you-PL-DIM-DUB eat-2pl
'they say he hit them, saying that you, that you just eat'

Here again /komi-ngichi/ 'you (pl.) eat', the verb in the domain of /ki/ or /ke/, receives ordinary main clause person marking. The same utterance contains an example of /-shka-/ complementation.

The compound P+ COMP /porke/ 'because' occurs with both main clause person marked verbs, as in /39/, and subordinate verbs, as in /40/:

/39/ todabia no byen aprendi-naku-n *porke* eskwela-bi anda-naku-*n*
still not well learn-PL-3 because school-LO walk-PL-3
'they don't learn well yet because they go to school'

/40/ *porke* no awa abi-*kpi* no kosecha-nchi
because not water be-SUB not harvest-1pl
'because there is no water we don't harvest'

In our ML sample, /aunke/ only occurs with subordinate verbs, as in /41/:

/41/ *aunke* duru llubi-xu-*kpi*-sh sali-gi-xu-ni-mi
though hard rain-PR-SUB-IND go-INC-PR-1sg-AF
'although it is raining hard I am going to go out'

Regarding the introduction into ML of the clause-initial complementizer /ki/ and its compound forms, we can conclude that: 1) they are relatively infrequent; 2) they sometimes introduce main clause person marked verbs, sometimes subordinate verbs; 3) they sometimes appear to be direct borrowings from Sp. On the whole, the Q system of nominal and adverbial marking on verbs to indicate subordination is the predominant type of complementation in ML. Possibly at a later stage the language will develop a regular clause-initial COMP position.

With the exception of embedded wh-questions and complementizers, where a large-scale syntactic change may be going on, the other instances of syntactic differences between Q and ML are minor and lexically induced. The claim that ML is a form of Q with Sp vocabulary can be maintained.

In Section 2 (Media Lengua) and in this section (Relexification and Its Consequences) we have seen a number of cases where there is variation within ML. This variation may have been caused by any or all of the following: 1) the variation is already present in the source language, Q; 2) the variation emerged within ML and has a stylistic nature; 3) the variation is due to different degrees of lexical adaptation to Sp (the axis relexification-translexification); and 4) the variation is due to borrowing or grammatical influence from Sp.

Variation Already Present in Q

An example of variation in ML, which also exists in Q, is variation in word order (see Table 7); sometimes objects and complements follow the verb, but more frequently they precede it. The CF sample is slightly more SOV than the other two samples. Another case of variation shared by ML and Q is the (redundant) marking with negative /-chu/, as in Table 9:

Table 9
Cases of Negative Main Clauses With and Without the Negation Marker /-chu/ (disregarding /no se/)

	CF	CI	MI	Total
with /-chu/	31	28	11	70
without /-chu/	12	64	23	99
% without /-chu/	28	69	68	59
(no se		11	2	13)

The CF sample, which was formally elicited, shows a much lower percentage of /-chu/ deletion (or absence of /-chu/ placement) than the CI and MI samples. No quantitative data are available on either Q word order or Q /-chu/ placement for comparison with the ML data of Tables 7 and 9.

Another case of variation involves the types of infinitival complements that certain verbs select, e.g., /kiri-/ 'wish' in Table 2. The comparable Q verb /muna-/ can also select /-na/, /-na-da/, /-y/, and /-nga-bu/ complements. This choice is mainly determined by consideration of style and emphasis; it has not yet been systematically investigated.

Stylistic Variation in ML Independent from Sp and Absent in Q

ML has developed several cases of variation involving the reduction of lexical items. Two cases in point are the alternation /yuya-ni/ ∿ /ya-ni/ 'I think', and the alternation /dizi-/ ∿ /zi-/ 'say, want'. When 'I think' is affixed to a statement, as a parenthetical, the result is /ya-ni/; otherwise, it is /yuya-ni/. Interestingly enough, the alternation is absent in Q (even though the verb /yuya-/ occurs in Q), and it is limited to the 1st person. The choice between /zi-/ (73 occurrences) and /dizi-/ (50 occurrences) seems to be determined by considerations of emphasis and lento/allegro style.

The existence of this type of variation in ML testifies to its long history and to its being the principal language of its speech community. If ML were a recent pidgin without native speakers, this type of variation would not be present.

Variation due to Different Degrees of Lexical Adaptation to Sp

When discussing the relexification of Q /riku-/ 'see' and forms derived from it, we noted that sometimes a strictly relexified form occurs (see Table 4 and example /15/) and sometimes a semantically complex form is adopted from Sp. In Table 10 we see the proportion of roots in the three ML samples compared with derived forms:

Table 10
The Proportion of Roots (including forms with /-xu-/ 'progressive' and /-naku-/ 'plural') to Derived Forms in the Three Samples

	CF	CI	MI	Total
roots	290	863	447	1600
derived forms	66	91	41	198
total	356	954	488	1798
% derived forms	18.6	9.5	8.4	11.0

The CF sample shows a considerably higher percentage of derived forms and is more "Q-like" than the other two samples.

We will discuss one more case of variation along this general axis relexification-translexification. This case involves locatives. In Q, locatives are formed by affixing locative case to deictic pronouns, whereas in Sp we find locative adverbs occurring by themselves. In ML we find no cases of strict relexification, that is, deictic pronouns with case markers. Instead we find the Sp locative adverbs /allá/, /akí/, /allí/, /ahí/, in 76 percent of the cases combined with a locative case marker:

Table 11
Locative Adverbs in the Three Samples

	CF	CI	MI	Total
allá		8	6	14
allá + case	2	16	12	30 (68%)
akí		5	6	11
akí + case	6	45	11	62 (85%)
allí		4	4	8
allí + case	1	11	5	17 (68%)
ahí		16	3	19
ahí + case		45	15	60 (75%)
Total Locative		33	19	52
Total Locative + Case	9	117	43	169
% Locative + Case	100%	78%	69%	76%

Again, CF is the most "Q-like," and the MI sample is slightly more "Sp-like" than the CI sample.

Variation due to Grammatical Influence from Sp

We have seen several cases where grammatical influence from Sp is a cause of variation in ML: the introduction of prepositions, conjunctions, complementizers, word order changes, etc. A major grammatical variable which so far has not been discussed is the subordinator /-ndu/. This is the only productive Sp affix which has been adopted in ML.

In Q, adverbial clauses (temporals, conditionals, concessives) are formed by adding either /-(k)pi/ 'obviative subordination' or /-sha/ 'proximate subordination' to the verb form:

/42a/ Q tamia-*kpi*-ga mana ri-sha-chu
rain-*kpi*-TO not go-1FU-NEG obviate
'if it rains I won't go'

/42b/ chaya-*sha*-mi miku-sha
arrive-*sha*-AF eat-1FU proximate
'I'll eat when I arrive'

In ML we find both /-kpi/ and /-sha/, but also /-ndu/ as an alternative to either:

/43/ ML ahi-bi toka-*ndu* isti sabi-nga-ma-bish
PRO-LOC play-*ndu* this know-3FU-IND-IND obviate
'if we play there this one will know'

/44/ bwenu uyari-xu-*kpi*-ga graba-nga-bu, disku-da
well hear-PR-*kpi*-TO record-NOM-BEN, record-AC obviate
'when they have heard it well, to record it, the record'

/45/ el-kuna-ga asi nustru abla-ri-k-ta-s uye-*ndu*-ga aprendi-n
he-PL-TO thus we talk-RE-NOM-AC hear-*ndu*-TO learn-3 proximate
'they learn it when they hear what we speak'

/46/ ahi-mi ya awanta-*sha* sinta-ri-naku-n
PRO-AF ya stand-*sha* live-RE-PL-3 proximate
'there they live together standing it'

Table 12 shows the distribution of /-kpi/, /-sha/, and /-ndu/ in the three samples, and the percentage of the /-ndu/ forms that are proximate:

Table 12
The Subordinating Suffixes /-ndu/, /-sha/, and /-kpi/ in the Three Samples

	CF	CI	MI	Total
-sha	5	18	23	46
-kpi	6	28	5	39
-ndu	9	95	52	156
% -ndu	45%	67%	65%	65%
% proximate	100%	85%	95%	92%

Again, we note that the CF sample, with fewer /-ndu/ forms, is more "Q-like" than the other two samples. Also we see that in the majority of cases /-ndu/ replaces /-sha/, not /-kpi/.

In this section we have attempted to give a technical definition of relexification; we have sketched some of the linguistic constraints under which relexification can take place; we have seen in which ways the syntax of ML diverges from that of Q; and finally, we have sketched some of the areas in which variation occurs in ML.

In the next section we will attempt to find an explanation for the emergence of ML, and we will try to put the notion of relexification in the general perspective of a theory of language genesis.

4. Why Relexification?

Why did Q speakers relexify their language and create ML? Most theories of pidgin (and hence creole) genesis assume that pidgins emerged through: 1) the need for communication among people with different language backgrounds; 2) processes of incomplete target language learning due to a quantitively restricted second language input; and 3) qualitative restrictions on the target language input through the use of foreigner talk registers by speakers of dominant groups. We will argue here that none of these processes contributed to the emergence of ML.

First of all, ML is an intra-group language, not known outside the communities where it is spoken. Given the fact that its structure is almost entirely Q, and that th vocabulary adopted from Sp has been both relexified and adapted to Q phonology, as the examples show, it is not any more intelligible to Sp speakers than to Q. In fact, few, if any, Sp speakers understand ML, while a substantial number of them have some knowledge of Q through contacts with Indians from different communities in the region. We have seen that some of the variation in ML is of a stylistic nature, and would tend to decrease intelligibility for Sp speakers.

Secondly, ML cannot be considered to represent a stage in learning Sp as a second language since many ML speakers also speak fluent Sp, and since ML is very different from Q-Sp interlanguage (cf. Muysken 1979). In Q-Sp interlanguage we find SOV word order, but no Q morphology, with the exception of the topic marker /-ga/. We also find very few cases of relexification, and no systematic adaptation of Sp vocabulary to Q phonology. Furthermore, if ML were the product of a process of second langauge learning, we would expect much more variation in the language than actually occurs.

Finally, regarding the relation between ML and Sp foreigner talk, it is very difficult to see a connection between the two since they share hardly any features. Sp foreigner talk is characterized by the use of infinitives, frequent diminutives, and a general reduction of Sp surface structures. Only coincidentally, as in the absence of articles (which are lacking also in Q), do we find a similarity with ML.

If these three causes are not responsible for the emergence of ML, how then can it be explained? We will suggest here that ML came into existence because acculturated Indians could not identify completely with either the traditional rural Q culture, or the urban Sp culture. Thus, it was not communicative needs that led to it, but rather expressive needs. It appears that ethnic self-identification is of crucial importance in determining the relation between Q, ML, and Sp in the Ecuadorian Highlands. ML is not the product of an interlanguage arrested and fixed, resulting from an emergency contact situation; but rather it is a departure from Q through massive relexification, and not at all along the path of Q-Sp interlanguage.

The ML-speaking community studied here is located on the fringe of a Qspeaking area, to which the community historically belonged. Due to its geographical situation and due to the necessity for and possibility of its inhabitants to make frequent trips to the capital to look for work, the community has come to be culturally differentiated from neighboring areas to the extent that its people find it necessary to set themselves apart from their neighbors.

The following comments on ML illustrate attitudes people hold toward the language:

/47/ Así se confundieron los vivientes, que por eso ha salido esta media lengua, porque no comprendieron bien ni el castellano ni el quichua.
'That way the people living [i.e., right after the Sp conquest] got confused, that's why that ML has come out, because they understood neither Q nor Sp very well'.

/48/ Entre nosotros no más hablamos, entre conocidos no más; los otros siempre hablan castellano. Sólo en este Cotopaxi hablan así. Las provincias otras no hablan, pero quichua no más.
'We just speak it among ourselves, among people we know; the others always speak Sp. Only in this province of Cotopaxi we talk like this. The other provinces don't speak it, only Q'.

/49/ ¿La Yolanda sí sabe algo de quichua, verdad?
Quichua grande no sabe, pero quichua chico ha aprendido donde su abuelita.
'Yolanda knows some Q, right?'
'Big Q [i.e., Q] she doesn't know, but little Q [i.e., ML] she has learned from her grandmother'.

/50/ Media Lengua-ga así Ingichu-munda Castellanu-da abla-na kiri-xu-sha,
ML-TO thus Q-from Sp-AC talk-NOM want-PR-SUB,
no abla-naku-ndu-mi asi, chaupi-ga Castellanu laya,
not talk-PL-SUB-AF thus, half-TO Sp like,
i chaupi-ga Ingichu laya abla-ri-na ga-n. Isi-ga asi nustru barrio-ga asi
and half-TO Q like talk-RE-NOM be-3. This-TO thus our community-TO thus
kostumbri-n abla-na.
accustomed-3 talk-NOM
'ML is thus if you want to talk Sp from Q, but you can't, then you talk half like Sp, and half like Q. In our community we are accustomed to talking this way'.

These comments illustrate: the sense of cultural indeterminacy (/47/); the private communal character of ML (/48/, /50/); and the position of ML halfway between Q and Sp (/49/, /50/).

If we assume that ML provides communities and individuals with a way of articulating their sense of cultural identity (an identity which cannot be fitted into the traditional, strict equations Q = Indian, Sp = White, which the caste society of the Ecuadorian Andes has provided), then the conservatism apparent in ML becomes more understandable. In Section 3 of this paper I have stressed the variability inherent in ML, but when one compares it with other Amerindian contact languages in Ecuador–such as Catalangu, spoken around Cañar–the surprising thing is its remarkable homogeneity. The samples CF and CI were collected in a completely different manner, yet they show many similarities, even when submitted to quantitative analysis.

It has been argued in this paper that relexification can play a major role in the emergence of a new language, and that the need for expression of an intermediate identity within a group can lead to the process of relexification. Most recent explanations of pidgin genesis have made two contrary assumptions: 1) that the primary *mechanism* involved in pidgin genesis is second language learning with a restricted input; and 2) that the primary *cause* of pidgin genesis is inter-group communication. Here I do not want to dispute the legitimacy of these assumptions, but rather I want to suggest that language genesis can take place along various paths: that of interrupted second language learning in inter-group communication, and that of relexification in intra-group communication.

A survey of recent literature on second language learning (e.g., Hatch 1978) shows that interference from the native language plays a relatively minor part in the acquisition of the syntax of a second language. If it is the case that the Caribbean creoles show numerous African survivals in their syntax and semantics, then I think we can argue that it is not interference which led to these survivals, but relexification. Adopting Alleyne's (1971) notion of creole genesis as acculturation, we could say that the Caribbean slaves spoke pidgin for inter-group communicative purposes, but at the same time relexified their native languages into the pidgin to express their new problematic cultural identity. They were not only Africans, but also slaves.

NOTES

1. Part of the research on Media Lengua was funded through a grant of the Netherlands Foundation for the Advancement of Tropical Research (WOTRO). I wish to thank numerous colleagues at the Institute for General Linguistics at the University of Amsterdam for comments on earlier versions, and L. R. Stark, P. A. Menges, D. Dilworth, P. Mühlhäusler, C. Lefebvre, and the people of Salcedo, Ecuador, for their help and encouragement.

2. Other varieties include a form of Media Lengua spoken near Saraguro, Joja; a contact language called Catalangu spoken around Cañar, Cañar; Cayapa Spanish spoken in parts of the province of Esmeraldas, Shuar Spanish spoken in the southern part of the Ecuadorian Amazon basin; and extinct forms of Záparo Spanish spoken in the central part of the Ecuadorian Amazon basin. Muysken (forthcoming) presents a sample of the different languages.

3. The orthography used to present the Q and ML samples is a modification of phonetic orthography:

b	=	voiced bilabial stop
ch	=	palatal stop
g	=	voiced velar stop
ll	=	palatalized lateral, sometimes pronounced fricatively
ñ	=	palatal nasal
sh	=	palatal fricative

4. The following abbreviations are used in the glosses:

AC	accusative
AF	affirmative
BEN	benefactive
DIM	diminutive
DUB	dubitative
FU	future tense
IND	indefinite
LOC	locative
NEG	negation marker
NOM	nominalizer
PA	past tense
pl	plural person
PL	plural
PR	progressive aspect
PRO	pronominal
RE	reflexive
sg	singular person
SUB	adverbial subordinator
TOP	topic marker

(ED: The generic term, Quechua, is used throughout this paper; the specific term used in Peru is Quechua, and in Ecuador it is Quichua.)

EXPANSION FONCTIONNELLE ET EVOLUTION

Gabriel Manessy
Université de Nice

1. Modèles d'évolution

1.1 Dans une étude récente (Valdman 1977a:70-98), E. C. Traugott a examiné les implications des recherches menées sur la pidginisation et la créolisation pour trois théories de l'évolution linguistique: celle qui fonde la méthode comparative historique élaborée par les Néo-grammairiens, celle qu'ont développée les générativistes et la théorie des ondes. Le cadre de notre exposé sera fourni par un autre modèle que E. C. Traugott n'a pas évoqué, le modèle fonctionnaliste dont l'initiateur est A. Martinet (1955, 1961, 1975). Il ne diffère guère, en ce qui concerne le principe du changement linguistique, du modèle générativiste qui est lui-même fort semblable, sur ce point, au modèle génétique: la langue se transforme parce qu'elle est inexactement transmise de génération en génération. Cette inexactitude est imputée à la négligence par les Néo-grammairiens, par les générativistes à l' aptitude des enfants à produire une grammaire plus simple, pour le même effet, que les adultes et à la tendance de ces derniers à compliquer la grammaire qu'ils ont formée dans leur enfance, et par les fonctionnalistes à une antinomie entre les exigences de la communauté qui réclame un instrument de communication à la fois souple et précis et la "tendance au moindre effort" qui porte chaque individu, dans la mesure où il échappe ou n'est pas encore soumis aux rigueurs de la norme sociale, à ne retenir de sa langue que ce qui est indispensable à une transmission efficace de l'information. Dans tous les cas, l'évolution est conçue comme une sorte de dérive qui n'est gouvernée que par le hasard des contacts avec des systèmes linguistiques étrangers.

1.2 Il est possible cependant, à l'intérieur du modèle fonctionnaliste, de concevoir une évolution qui ne soit point aveugle. Les recherches sociolinguistiques ont mis en évidence la multiplicité des variétés qui constituent normalement le répertoire d'une communauté et la complémentarité, au moins partielle, des fonctions qui leur sont assignées. On peut concevoir qu'il existe une corrélation entre la fonction primaire qu'assume telle variété de langue et ses caractéristiques proprement linguistiques. La spécialisation dans le rôle de code de communication, utilisé principalement pour la transmission de messages faisant référence au "contexte" (Jakobson 1963:213), a pour effet une fonctionnalisation des moyens d'expression linguistique dans le sens où ce terme est employé, en technologie comparée, pour décrire l'évolution de la forme des outils: plus d'efficacité pour une moindre dépense d'énergie. Ce processus aboutit à la constitution de variétés véhiculaires dont les pidgins, exempts de toute connotation normative ou catégorisante, représentent l'état le plus achevé. Réciproquement une variété qui se trouve investie de l'ensemble des valeurs reconnues par la communauté, dont l'emploi est perçu comme une célébration de la personnalité ethnique, subit une élaboration, tant au niveau morphophonologique qu'à celui des structures grammaticales, qui tout à la fois garantit l'exactitude de la liturgie sociale et authentifie les droits qu'ont ses usagers à y participer.

1.3 Ces deux tendances opposées peuvent rendre compte de cas où l'évolution semble s'orienter dans une direction définie, comme si la transformation du système linguistique cessait d'avoir pour unique fin le rétablissement d'un équilibre perpétuellement compromis; mais elles n'impliquent qu'un seul et même principe d'explication: la restriction et la spécification du champ fonctionnel. Notre propos est d'examiner ici ce qui se passe dans le cas inverse, c'est-à-dire lorsque le champ fonctionnel d'une variété s'élargit de telle sorte que celle-ci devienne utilisable dans un plus grand nombre de situations. C'est à la multiplication des fonctions qu'on impute habituellement le déclenchement des processus de complexification et d'élaboration désignés globalement par le terme de créolisation. Nous pensons que ceci est une condition nécessaire plutôt que suffisante à la constitution d'un créole et que cette extension, lorsqu'elle n'est pas liée à la formation d'une communauté close (c'est-à-dire dans la mesure où la fonction intégrative n'est pas prédominante) conduit à un type de variété que nous appellerons, en détournant par commodité le vocable de son acception stylistique habituelle, "vernaculaire," le processus linguistique dont elle résulte étant dit "vernacularisation."

2. Français d'Afrique

2.1 La vernacularisation est sans doute un phénomène fort commun, mais peu décrit. On doit s'attendre à le trouver plus aisément observable dans une situation de plurilinguisme où le répertoire de la communauté juxtapose des variétés ressortissant à des systèmes linguistiques différents, où les chevauchements sont plus manifestes et les limites de la variabilité plus faciles à tracer. L'objet de notre étude sera donc la formation, souvent postulée, mais pratiquement jamais analysée jusqu'à ce jour de français régionaux en Afrique.

L'étude porte sur un corpus de français oral (Manessy 1978), recueilli entre juin 1977 et janvier 1978 dans le Sud du Cameroun, par C. de Féral. Les informateurs principaux sont au nombre de vingt-cinq, hommes et femmes, leur âge variant entre cinq et plus de soixante-dix ans, appartenant à des milieux différents (journalistes, instituteurs, fonctionnaires, commerçants, chauffeurs de taxi, manoeuvres, employés de maison, ménagères), pour moitié scolarisés, les autres ayant acquis le français par apprentissage direct. Il s'agit dans la plupart des cas de conversation familières entre l'enquêteur, C. de Féral ou l'un de ses collaborateurs camerounais, et les informateurs sur des sujets touchant à la vie quotidienne ou à la biographie de chacun; figurent en outre dans le corpus l'interview à la radio d'un homme d'affaires (non-lettré) et un interrogatoire au commissariat de police. Ces textes donnent, au premier examen, une impression de grande confusion; certains se présentent comme des imitations plus ou moins fidèles de la langue scolaire, ou administrative, d'autres comme des enchaînements incohérents de phrases mal formées et souvent incomplètes; tous les intermédiaires peuvent êtres trouvés entre l'expression correcte et le charabia incompréhensible, mais il n'est guère d'enregistrement qui ne comporte l'un et l'autre en diverses proportions. Toutefois, le désarroi du métropolitain n'est apparemment pas partagé par les locuteurs du français camerounais: il est manifeste qu'un sujet capable d'user d'un français proche du standard n'est pas déconcerté par le discours, pour nous partiellement inintelligible, de son interlocuteur illettré, quoique la réciproque ne soit pas totalement vraie. Il apparaît d'autre part que la variété la plus semblable au français métropolitain en diffère par des particularités difficiles à identifier. Prises individuellement, la plupart des constructions peuvent trouver leur caution dans un usage de la langue courante, mais les énoncés qu'elles constituent donnent un sentiment d'étrangeté qui ne résulte que très partiellement du mélange, souvent signalé, des styles. La bizarrerie s'accroît à mesure qu'on s'éloigne de l'usage des lettrés, mais elle devient moins troublante parce qu'on se croit alors autorisé à l'imputer aux effets d'un apprentissage imparfait. Un examen plus attentif suggère une interprétation propre à rendre compte de l'ensemble de ces faits: tout se passe comme si les locuteurs du français camerounais disposaient d'une grammaire commune, non identique à celle de la variété standard, seule présente chez les sujets dont la compétence en français est la plus rudimentaire, mais encore décelable chez les autres où elle semble constituer la base sur laquelle se fondent les approximations plus ou moins cohérentes, en direction de la norme scolaire. Il est probable que nombre d'énoncés que l'observateur métropolitain reconnaît pour corrects ne le sont qu'en apparence, en vertu d'une ambiguïté de surface qui masque une structure aberrante. Nous en prendrons pour exemple le cas des propositions enchâssées, relatives et complétives.

2.2 Modifications grammaticales

2.2.1 La règle qui, dans le corpus, gouverne la construction des propositions relatives est simple: la proposition est introduite par *qui* si le substantif qu'elle détermine a le même référent que son propre sujet, par *que* dans le cas contraire: *ce sont les gens d'ici qui gâté notre pays;... si je vois quelqu'un que je veux aller me marier*... Le premier énoncé est conforme en apparence à la norme standard (mise à part la forme du verbe), le second est manifestement incorrect: on attendrait *avec qui.* En réalité, l'"incorrection" ne se situe pas au niveau morphophonologique: *que* n'est aucunement pronom et n'assume aucune fonction dans la proposition relative; en témoignent des énoncés tels que: *tout ce que j'en ai besoin, je pars donner ce que je l'avais pris* où le complément du verbe *(en, l(e))* est explicitement exprimé. La référence indue à la norme risque d'engendrer le contresens: *le petit bombe là qu'on lance* n'est pas un engin explosif, mais un "atomiseur" qui sert à projeter *(lancer)* un liquide pulvérisé. *Que* n'est qu'une particule de liaison, présente aussi dans la forme *qui* que l'on a toutes raisons de considérer comme un amalgame *que + i(l),* d'ailleurs parfois explicitement décomposé: *je reçois surtout ma première femme qu'il est tout à fait lettré,* et dont la structure apparaît clairement lorsque *il* commute avec *ça: je ne sais pas ce que ça va se passer là-bas.*

Le français standard possède une conjonction, *que,* homophone de la forme objet du pronom relatif, qui introduit des propositions complétives. On trouverait sans peine dans le corpus nombre d'exemples de telles complétives "correctement" employées après des verbes tels que *dire, connaître* (au sens de *savoir*), *vouloir,* etc.; mais on rencontre aussi, fréquemment, des expressions telles que: *il a refusé qu'il ne va pas m'épouser, ses soeurs m'ont retenue que j'allais accoucher* où la complétive ne peut pas être considérée comme le complément d'objet du verbe principal. Pour les interpréter, il faut tenir compte de ce que le verbe ne comporte pas dans la variété considérée le trait [+/– transitif] ; tout verbe peut être employé absolument: *moi je sais seulement ici à Yaoundé* (je n'ai d'informations que sur ce qui se passe à Yaoundé), ou être accompagné de déterminants qui en précisent l'acception: d'où des locutions telles que *travailler le manoeuvre* (être employé comme manoeuvre), *sortir la route* (aller dans la rue), *fonctionner chauffeur* (être chauffeur fonctionnaire). Le rapport syntaxique entre la proposition complétive et le verbe principal est analogue à celui qui existe entre *travailler* et *le manoeuvre; que* n'a d'autre fonction que de marquer cette relation comme il le fait dans le cas de la proposition "relative," la seule différence étant que dans un cas c'est un nom et dans l'autre un verbe qui se trouvent déterminés. Le même mécanisme s'applique là où le français standard use de deux transformations distinctes, relative et complétive.

2.2.2 On pourrait produire d'autres exemples qui illustrent l'allègement de l' appareil syntaxique. La caractéristique dominante du français camerounais est la prééminence de l'intention sémantique sur les contraintes grammaticales. Celles-ci ne sont habituellement prévalentes que dans un style soutenu; dans tous les autres cas, elles sont respectées dans la mesure où elles ne contredisent pas la logique du discours et l'expression se modèle sur la forme du contenu. Cela est manifeste en ce qui concerne les règles de concordance des modes et des temps; des énoncés tels que: *c'est moi même qui lui avais demandé s'il va* (s'il allait) *me marier* sont courants. L'emploi du subjonctif est lié à l'expression de la finalité; la même informateur dit: *Je ne faisais que faire la malignité pour qu'elles ne sachent pas que je sens mal,* ce qui est conforme à la règle, et: *j'avais supporté et préparé jusqu'à ce que les invitées sont* (soient) *venues,* qui ne l'est pas. Le choix des prépositions est largement aléatoire, mais dans la mesure où il obéit à une règle, celle-ci est sémantique: *chez le domicile* (au domicile), *avec cette bagarre* (en ce qui concerne cette bagarre), *marcher sur le soleil* (au soleil). Un procédé très commun consiste à expliciter le constituant de phrase affirmatif *(c'est (que))* au même titre que l'interrogatif *(est-ce que): Ouais, si vous êtes bien, ça va. C'est que moi aussi je suis bien.* A un niveau plus profond, le système même de la langue semble avoir été remanié, du moins en certaines de ses parties. L'opposition fondamentale, en ce qui concerne le verbe, paraît être entre un terme non-marqué, réalisé par une forme dérivée de l'infinitif chez les sujets les moins compétents, par celle du présent de l'indicatif chez les autres, et des termes marqués pour le passé (formes du passé composé, de l'imparfait ou du plus-que-parfait de l'indicatif en variation libre) et le futur (au moyen de l'auxiliaire *aller,* parfois *vouloir*). Les sujets les plus compétents sont capables d'employer correctement les temps s'ils surveillent leur langage—c'est-à-dire d'opérer une discrimination entre imparfait (passé + durée), passé composé (passé accompli) et plus-que-parfait (antériorité dans le passé)—mais le système élémentaire reparaît dès que leur vigilance se relâche.

2.2.3 Il ne saurait être question d'imputer les particularités du français camerounais à un quelconque substrat; outre que celui-ci est, au Cameroun, fort différencié, S. Lafage (1976) fait, à propos du français togolais parlé en pays ewe, des remarques tout à fait analogues, notamment en ce qui concerne l'emploi de *que* (1976:129), celui des prépositions (1976:417, 567), les temps du verbe (1976:500) ou sa définition lexicale (1976:623). On aurait peine à trouver des langues typologiquement plus différentes que l'ewe et les parlers bantou. Force est donc de reconnaître dans ces phénomènes de simplification et de réduction l'équivalent de ce qu'on désigne ailleurs par le terme de pidginisation. Le français camerounais est loin cependant de présenter la rigidité qu'on impute aux variétés véhiculaires. Sa flexibilité stylistique est indéniable, mais elle est assurée par d' autres moyens que la manipulation des ressources grammaticales. Le vocabulaire y tient une grande place. Dans toute l'Afrique francophone, la compétence en français se mesure au nombre des mots dont dispose le locuteur et à la diversité des sujets sur lesquels il peut discourir (le contenu du discours étant d'importance tout à fait secondaire). Cela donne lieu à des joutes oratoires, entre adolescents surtout. Un autre critère d'évaluation est l'aisance manifestée dans le maniement de la langue; les attributs en sont la rapidité et la fluidité de l'élocution et l'abondance du discours beaucoup plus que son exactitude; la redondance pallie l'impropriété des termes et l'imprécision des construction grammaticales et assure l'intelligibilité globale. Il semble que ce soit là une manifestation constante de la prise de possession d'une variété de langue par ses locuteurs; Poutignat et Wald (1978) signalent le même phénomène pour le sango urbain et Richardson (1961) pour le Town Bemba. L'intérêt réside dans sa signification: il implique la dissolution du lien entre la norme prescriptive et la validité de l'usage. L'efficacité communicative l'emporte sur le souci de correction grammaticale; l'insécurité linguistique qu'implique l'emploi d'une variété "haute" dans les fonctions qui lui sont normalement assignées se trouve ici abolie. Une autre conséquence de cette neutralisation est la très large tolérance à l'égard des variations individuelles. L'ampleur de ces variations, et surtout le fait que leur champ d'action empiète parfois sur le domaine de systèmes linguistiques distincts ont déconcerté plus d'un linguiste. Le problème n'est pas proprement africain. G. Hazaël-Massieux (1978:106) traitant de la diglossie français-créole en Guadeloupe montre à quel point les typologies linguistiques et sociolinguistiques communes sont impuissantes à rendre compte du fonctionnement de communautés "dont la cohésion est manifestée par la volonté d'intelligibilité mutuelle plutôt que par l'unité évidente d'un système linguistique." Il y a en Guadeloupe *un* parler vernaculaire, où français et créole sont indifférenciés en ce qu'on ne peut sans arbitraire en imputer les énoncés à l'une ou l'autre de ces langues, et le recours au français standard ou à un créole épuré marque toujours une prise de distance, la revendication d'un statut particulier au sein de la communauté ou la volonté de s'en exclure.

2.3 Conventions de discours

2.3.1 Si peu structurée que soit une communauté–et celle que constituent les utilisateurs du français camerounais l'est infiniment moins que la société créole dont parle G. Hazaël-Massieux–elle dispose du moins d'indices par lesquels ses membres s'identifient comme tels et se reconnaissent entre eux. Dans le cas examiné, certains de ces indices sont certainement paralinguistiques; il s'agit d'un certain "habitus" verbal: prononciation, intonation, mimique, et de l'emploi de certains procédés expressifs, tel l'allongement de la voyelle finale de l'adverbe dans *je l'ai attendu depuis* [dəpɥi:::] (pendant très longtemps); mais il semble bien que d'autres traits, plus strictement linguistiques, soient en voie de codification et que quiconque manque à les employer, ou les emploie hors de propos, se dénonce comme étranger. Le discours des usagers du français camerounais, à tous les niveaux de compétence, comporte la récurrence incessante d'un petit nombre d'adverbes et de locutions: *même, là, comme ça, comme ça là, c'est-à-*

dire, mais, aussi. L'examen du corpus montre que la distribution de ces termes n'est que rarement conforme aux règles qui régissent leur emploi en français standard, mais qu'elle n'est pas pour autant aléatoire. Leur contenu est difficile à déterminer: *aussi* a valeur assertive, il atteste l'authenticité de ce qui est affirmé: *"Mon nom aussi c'est Colette," "je n'étais pas là; j'étais à l'hôpital, je suis aussi rentrée avant que j'aie su qu'on a déposé une plainte." Même* est également assertif, mais son rôle est analogue à celui du soulignement dans l'écriture, ou du corps italique en typographie: il met en évidence le membre de phrase où il est inséré, ou le vocable auquel il est accolé: *"Où toi tu te trouvais, où même . . . ?"* Sa fonction démarcative apparaît dans l'énoncé suivant, à structure paratactique, où la première proposition évoque une situation imaginaire et les autres les comportements qu'elle implique: *"Même mon frère vient comme ça, hein, tu lui donnes même 500, même 2000. Même tu lui donnes un vin rouge." Mais* appartient au même groupe, il n'a aucunement la valeur adversative que lui reconnaît l'usage standard; c'est un déterminant affirmatif de la proposition; à la question *"Et vous comptez vous marier?"* une jeune femme répond *"Oui, mais on compte se marier"* (français standard: on compte bien se marier). *Là, comme ça, comme ça là* fonctionnent comme "embrayeurs" en ce qu'ils "renvoient au message" (Jakobson 1963:176); ils font référence à ce qui a été mentionné ou à un savoir implicite commun au locuteur et à son auditoire: ainsi dans le récit que fait une jeune femme de son accouchement: *"Ça me faisait comme ça, je poussais, ça ne sortait pas, arrivé à un moment là, comme ça là, cela m'a attaqué à me faire toujours fort . . ."* ou encore dans cette question d'un inspecteur au témoin qui vient de déclarer qu'il habitait *"chez son papa": "Comment s'appelle votre papa là?" C'est-à-dire* introduit au contraire un complément d'information explicite soit sous forme de glose ou de paraphrase: *"Est-ce que tu sais que ça entraîne automatiquement quelqu'un à des peines privatives de liberté? C'est-à-dire que tu sais que cette affaire telle qu'elle est peut nous amener . . . à envoyer ce monsieur au parquet et là-bas il peut gagner une prison"* (avoir une peine de prison). Il n'est pas assuré que cette analyse soit exacte; mais l'usage de la trentaine de locuteurs représentés dans le corpus paraît cohérent et il existe certainement en cette matière des règles que devrait acquérir celui qui prétendrait parler le français comme un vrai Camerounais. Il s'agit bien là de procédés, certes non syntaxiques, mais servant "à la mise en relief ou à l'intensification, à la connotation subjective plutôt qu'à la dénotation objective" par lesquels se manifeste, selon Valdman (1978a:46), l'élaboration linguistique.

2.3.2 Le cas de *là* est particulièrement intéressant. Il est d'emploi fréquent en français populaire métropolitain: "ce garçon-là," "qu'est-ce que vous me racontez là," mais la fréquence de son emploi est une des caractéristiques les plus frappantes du français d'Afrique. S. Lafage (1976:387), parlant du français togolais, y voit "un véritable tic de langage" et met cet usage en rapport avec l'existence en ewe, langue du substrat, d'une modalité de rappel *a* ou *là* (l'accent grave notant ici le ton bas) suffixée au nom. Il est vraisemblable que cette coïncidence a beaucoup contribué à la systématisation de l'emploi de *là* après le substantif, en tant qu' "article emphatique, invariable, postposé": *ballon là, c'est raté,* qui toutefois n'exclut pas la présence de l'article défini: *l' garçon là, il est fort; je connais la femme là,* et qui n'est pas obligatoire: *le père m'a crié* (mon père m'a grondé). D'autre part, la distribution de *là* n'est pas limitée à la position post-nominale; on le trouve aussi en fin de proposition: *c'est son moteur il est gâté là* (son vélomoteur ne marche plus). La situation est tout à fait analogue en français populaire d'Abidjan, selon J. L. Hattiger (1978:16), où *là* postposé "accompagne non seulement le substantif, mais aussi d'autres catégories grammaticales: verbe, adverbe, adjectif": *mais quand depuis i finit là . . .* (mais depuis qu'il est mort . . .); *Tous ceux qui i gagné des enfants beaucoup là vous souffrez* (tous ceux qui ont beaucoup d'enfants ont une vie difficile); *y a beaucoup qui font le petit commerce là* (il y en a beaucoup qui pratiquent le petit commerce). Le français camerounais, où l'influence des langues (bantou) de substrat est dans le cas présent hors de question, produit des énoncés tout à fait analogues: . . . *comme ce qu'on appelle dzumba là, hein, en pidgin; il peut quand même comprendre quelques mots là; je fais la bouillon. Avant de faire la bouillon là, je écrase la tomate.* Comme au Togo, et comme en Côte d'Ivoire, l'article défini subsiste habituellement, quoiqu'à titre facultatif, devant le substantif, mais sa présence n'implique aucune détermination: *j'avais la grossesse de six mois; vous avez le domicile avec qui?;. . . et mon mari aussi il part au travail, oui. Dans gendarmerie.* Si la forme doit être marquée, elle l'est pour l'indéterminé par *un, une, des,* et pour le déterminé par *là* ou par une des particules ou locutions qui font référence au contexte: *j'ai accouché le garçon-ci; il y a maintenant les affaires comme ça là.*

2.3.3 Valdman (1976a:14; 1978a:50) constate que, dans le domaine des déterminants nominaux, les seuls traits partagés par l'ensemble des parlers francocréoles "résident dans un déterminant indéfini préposé . . . et un actualisant du nom postposé, se réalisant partout sous la forme *la,"* qui subit d'ailleurs dans les variétés antillaises une profonde complexification morphophonologique. La formation de ce "système conservateur" (par rapport à celui qu'on trouve aux Antilles), attesté en Louisiane, en Guyane et dans l'Océan Indien et qui est caractérisé d'autre part par l'antéposition des déterminants démonstratifs et possessifs et du marqueur pluriel, peut être, selon l'auteur, illustré par le système d'actualisation du syntagme nominal en français populaire d'Abidjan (F.P.A.) où "il s'est formé un système symétrique de déterminants de très grande simplicité dans lequel le déictique locatif *là* sert d'actualisateur et où le nombre est indiqué par le choix entre *lui* et *leur* postposé" (1978:53). Il est à remarquer que Hattiger n'a pas trouvé trace dans son corpus (oral) de cet emploi des pronoms personnels (1978a:15), la pluralité étant en revanche fréquemment indiquée par la postposition d'un adverbe de quantité, et que *là* n'y est pas confiné au rôle d'actualisateur du nom. Le désaccord s'explique aisément par le fait que Valdman a disposé, ainsi qu'il le fait observer, d'un corpus d'un type particulier: une chronique humoristique publiée dans un quotidien d'Abidjan et deux disques contenant une adaptation de textes de la Genèse. Il s'agit de l'ouvrage d'intellectuels francophones écrivant ou parlant pour d'autres lettrés, usagers occasionnels du français populaire, mais à qui cette capacité, partagée, procure un sentiment de connivence, de solidarité. Les rubriques patoisantes, dans les journaux régionaux de la métropole, assument la même fonction. Il est vraisemblable cependant que la systématisation porte sur des traits–en l'occurrence la présence récurrente de *là* après le substantif–que les locuteurs tiennent inconsciemment pour caractéristiques de leur parler: le F.P.A. de Valdman représente par rapport à celui de Hattiger et au français d'Afrique en général un degré supérieur d'élaboration, correspondant à celui qui est attesté dans le système conservateur des créoles français. Il semble que l'on saisisse ici le mécanisme par lequel un usage, du fait probablement qu'il est ressenti comme propre à un groupe de locuteurs, se stabilise et s'intègre au système de la langue.

3. Vernacularisation et évolution

3.1 Vernacularisation

Il paraît maintenant possible de donner de la vernacularisation une définition plus précise: il s'agit de l'effet produit par l'opération, sur une variété de langue, de deux processus complémentaires: la simplification des structures grammaticales et l'élaboration compensatoire des moyens d'expression. La simplification peut être, en quelque sorte, donnée d'avance; tel est le cas lorsque l'appropriation s'exerce sur une variété véhiculaire, comme cela se produit pour le sango en Centrafrique (Poutignat and Wald 1978), le lingala au Zaïre (Sesep N'Sial 1978) ou le pidgin-english au Nigeria (Obilade 1977). Elle résulte, dans le cas du français d'Afrique comme dans celui des koinès africaines, du relâchement de la tradition socioculturelle qui libère la langue des contraintes normatives. Ce qu'il y a de commun à toutes ces situations est que l'emploi de la variété simplifiée est interprété non comme un simple moyen d'intercompréhension, mais comme l'expression d'une solidarité qui transcende les différenciations ethniques et dont le cadre peut être la ville, la région, comme c'est le cas pour le peul dans le Sud-Ouest de la République du Tchad (Manessy 1978a:102) et peut être pour le français au Cameroun méridional (Renaud 1976), ou bien l'Etat, comme on le constate actuellement en Centrafrique pour le sango. Cette solidarité est manifestée par la communauté des conventions de discours. Il est aisé de concevoir comment, dans la mesure où le groupe des usagers se structure et s'organise et où s'affirment les fonctions interactive et rituelle du langage (Valdman 1978a:45), les usages peuvent se muer en règles, de telle sorte que ce qui n'était que procédé expressif (comme l'emploi de *là* en français d'Afrique) devienne hors contexte l'expression d'une catégorie grammaticale, telle que *là,* modalité nominale de détermination en créole français.

3.2 Vernacularisation et créolisation

L'intérêt de la notion de vernacularisation, qui exigerait certes une élaboration plus complète et peut être différente de celle que nous avons esquissée, est double. Elle fournit une réponse possible à certaines questions que pose l'interprétation des faits de pidginisation et de créolisation. Valdman (1977:175) écrit: "An important question in pidgin and creole linguistics is the degree of elaboration undergone by the terminus a quo of existing creoles" et il fait référence au problème posé par Alleyne (1971:172): si l'on admet la filiation entre les créoles français et anglais et leurs "langues de base," on est forcé de constater que la créolisation s'est effectuée sur des états de langue qui avaient été syntaxiquement remaniés, mais qui n'avaient été que fort peu altérés au niveau morphophonologique. Telle est à peu près l'image que nous offre le français d'Afrique dans ses emplois vernaculaires: une structure grammaticale réduite et un appareil morphologique surabondant dont chaque locuteur se sert avec une exactitude qui est à la mesure de sa capacité à imiter la norme. De même deux des "suggested field for research" du mémorandum de Reinecke (1971:500) ressortissent au domaine de la vernacularisation: "4. *Semi-pidginization.* Under what circumstances do some languages undergo extreme simplification . . . while others are only slightly simplified (Town Bemba, probably Kingwana Swahili, Bazaar Hindustani, Low Malay)? – 5. Circumstances under which languages suffer a rapid simplification of the sort which we generally attribute to trade contacts or similar superficial contacts in the case of recognized pidgins, but where speakers of the simplified languages are in intimate, continuous and non-discriminatory contact . . . ." Ce que notre corpus révèle est en effet une "semi-pidginization"; le français vernaculaire du Cameroun pas plus que le bemba urbain ou le swahili de Lubumbashi (cf. Rossé 1977) ne peuvent être tenus pour des pidgins, ni pour des créoles, et ils doivent leurs particularités linguistiques précisément au fait qu'ils sont employés par des gens en contact intime, continu, non-discriminatoire qui en usent comme d'une variété neutre quant aux connotations ethniques et sociales, pour les besoins que suscite une cohabitation quotidienne, celle-ci impliquant à son tour un mode de vie, des intérêts et des soucis partagés, des représentations communes dont le vernaculaire est l'expression.

3.3 Evolution

La notion de vernacularisation permet d'autre part de proposer une interprétation de ce que Alleyne (1971:171) désigne par "regular slow historical change" et que nous avions qualifié plus haut de "dérive." Il suffit d'admettre qu'à l'intérieur d'une communauté linguistique définie par la possession d'un même idiome et d'un même patrimoine socioculturel se produit un double mouvement. L'un, qui répond au besoin qu'éprouve la communauté de célébrer ce qui fonde son unité et la distingue de toutes les autres, consiste en une élaboration, c'est-à-dire en l'actualisation systématique des potentialités du système linguistique propres à permettre la différenciation des styles, et en l'imposition de contraintes normatives dont l'observation authentifie l'appartenance du locuteur au groupe. Ce processus peut être aisément observé dans des sociétés africaines attachées à leurs traditions, comme l'est la société peule (Labatut 1976), mais il aboutit tout aussi bien, en France et ailleurs, à la définition d'une langue académique, modèle vénéré et pratiquement inusité. L'autre mouvement est d'adaptation de la variété "haute" aux nécessités de l'usage quotidien; n'ayant pas les mêmes exigences de rigueur que la communication abstraite, celui-ci n'implique pas le maniement de mécanismes syntaxiques subtils et prend largement appui sur le "contexte," mais supposant une connivence entre les interlocuteurs, il demeure soumis à des conventions d'usage qui en garantissent la valeur intégrative. A mesure que la variété haute se fige dans sa fonction normative, le domaine du vernaculaire s'étend, les conventions se fixent et deviennent à leur tour objet d'élaboration. L'usage populaire devient le bon usage, l'ancienne variété haute est réputée désuète, puis archaïque et un nouveau vernaculaire se constitue. Cette vue simpliste, comme l'est tout modèle, de l'évolution a du moins le mérite de rendre compte, dans une perspective fonctionnaliste, de la résistance qu'oppose le "système" à des innovations qui devraient en principe conduire à une meilleure économie de la langue (au sens où l'entend Martinet: une plus grande efficacité dans la transmission du message pour un moindre coût). Ce système n'est point une entité abstraite; il correspond à la grammaire dont usent, à un moment donné, ceux dont le comportement linguistique est jugé conforme aux impératifs de la tradition socioculturelle. Cette grammaire est habituellement celle que les linguistiques descriptivistes prennent pour objet de leur analyse, aux dépens d'autres qui sont également constitutives de l'idiome; l'affirmation de l'hétérogénéité foncière de la langue est une des contributions majeures de la sociolinguistique à l'intelligence des faits d'évolution. Ce parti-pris n'est pourtant pas sans justification: c'est à partir du système de la langue "correcte" que peuvent être le plus aisément décelées les complications et les simplifications possibles. Une différence importante entre la vernacularisation et la pidginisation proprement dite est que les effets de la première ne sont pas aussi radicaux que peuvent l'être ceux de la seconde, dont il a été souvent supposé qu'elle mettait à jour certaines des structures élémentaires du langage humain. Dans le corpus français examiné, le système verbal conserve la base "chronologique" qu'il a en français standard; les relations entre propositions sont souvent exprimées par parataxe ou par des moyens lexicaux, mais trois "conjonction": *si, quand* et *parce (que)* demeurent d'usage courant. Le postulat structuraliste selon lequel le système réagit selon sa logique propre n'est pas mis en question par le mode d'interprétation que nous avons suggéré.

RESUME

1. **Modèles d'évolution.** Trois modèles: génétique, générativiste et dynamique ont été réexaminés par E. C. Traugott (in Valdman 1977) en fonction des résultats de recherches récentes sur la pidginisation et la créolisation. On se propose d' étendre l'étude au modèle structuraliste qui voit dans l'ajustement du système linguistique à des fonctions changeantes le principe de son évolution. La modification des fonctions peut se faire dans le sens d'une plus grande spécialisation ou par extension.

2. **Français d'Afrique.** Les effets de l'extension du champ fonctionnel d'une variété de langue, ici désignés par le terme de "vernacularisation," sont observés dans un corpus de français oral recueilli dans le Sud du Cameroun. On y constate un allègement de l'appareil syntaxique, une réduction des contraintes grammaticales et, de façon complémentaire, une systématisation des conventions de discours. Dans ce dernier domaine, le cas du déterminant postposé *là,* caractéristique des parlers franco-créoles, est plus particulièrement étudié.

3. **Vernacularisation.** Une définition provisoire de la vernacularisation est suggérée. Il est montré en quoi cette notion peut contribuer à élucider le problème du *terminus a quo* de la créolisation, rendre compte des cas de pidginisation incomplète et permettre de mieux comprendre, dans une perspective fonctionnaliste, le mécanisme d'évolution du système de la langue.

GUADELOUPEAN CREOLE PRONOUNS:
A Study of Expansion in Morphosyntactic Structure

Raleigh Morgan, Jr.
University of Michigan

1. Introduction

French-based creoles and popular French of the colonial period share basic lexicon and certain phonological features, as well as morphosyntax. Yet Valdman (1978a:386) would claim that it is precisely in morphosyntax that creole has drawn the clearest line between itself and French, making creole a *langue à part entière* and not a dialect of French. This relatively stable line of demarcation may explain why creoles–most of which are still in close contact with French–do not show post-creole features to the same extent that English-based creoles do. As for the cause of this structural rupture, Valdman would doubtlessly agree with Mühlhäusler (1979:20) that linguistic universals will be the main source of such changes in the areas of syntax and morphology, even if we do not completely discount influence from French or the learner's native language. Valdman (1977b) demonstrates this morphosyntactic integrity of creoles in his discussion of the noun determiner and verb particle systems.

In this article I claim that: 1) morphosyntactic patterns in the pronominal subsystems of Guadeloupean Creole (hereafter GC) show a variety of developmental changes (syntactic complexification, expanded derivational patterns); and 2) a comparison of equivalent data in other creoles as well as that of an earlier period of GC will bring more sharply into focus the extent to which such expansion in GC has not affected the structural integrity of that dialect.[1]

2. Personal Pronouns

The system of personal pronouns in French-based creoles is clearly derivable from their French counterparts, although morphophonemic alternations and functions may differ. For the first person, with an underlying *moi* as the source, Louisiana and Indian Ocean creoles are said to be the only varieties with subject and object forms. But this is also true for GC, which has *an* and *mwen,* although Germain (1976:77) considers *an* to be a reduced form of *mwen.* Examples include: *an ka ba-i ta-i* 'je lui donne le sien', *ba-mwen-i* 'donne-le-moi'. In other creoles there may be variation in form, but only one base form is posited. French-based creoles do not usually have the formal/informal distinction (T/V) for the second person, although Poyen-Bellisle (1894:39f.) does posit such a system for GC based on the contrast *to/twé* versus polite *ou* for 2sg. For 2pl., *zòt* is used. In the animal tale published by Poyen-Bellisle, the king addresses the rabbit with the *to* forms; and the latter, in turn, uses *ou* to address the king. In the case of 3sg., *li* or its truncated form is found in all creoles, i.e., *i* as subject and as post-vocalic object, but with *li* as post-consonantal object, after the copula *sé* and pre-pausally: *i tann li* 'il l'attend', *ban mwen-i* 'donne-le-moi', *an konpwann ka-i yé* 'je comprends ce qu'il est', *sé li ki ka ban mwen sa* 'c'est lui que me le donne'.

For modern usage, Germain (1976:77) shows certain changes. The situation for *(l)i* is similar to that described by Poyen-Bellisle, but for 2sg., 2pl., we find *ou* and *zò(t)*, respectively. However, my Guadeloupean assistant indicated that among some speakers, the *ou/vou* contrast in formality is maintained.

3. Demonstrative Pronouns

More complex are the demonstrative, relative, possessive, and indefinite pronoun systems. Goodman provides an excellent overview of these types. In his study (1964:50-53) of Creole French dialects, he includes, among his comparative etymologies, the creole reflexes of the French demonstratives *ça* and *cela.* We learn that both American and Indian Ocean creoles have a single demonstrative *sa,* meaning both 'this' and 'that', and that this pronoun is used as a substitute for any noun, animate or inanimate, singular or plural. The demonstrative *sa* has developed additional roles in creole, as we shall soon see. In addition to *sa,* there are other demonstratives, e.g., *sila* in Louisiana, Haitian, and Antillean creoles. In Haitian Creole (hereafter HC), the contrast *sa/sila-a* is seen by some as evidence of a proximity contrast (Goodman 1964:51, Sylvain 1936:58). Others interpret HC *sila-a* as having a deictic value for inanimate nouns (Valdman 1978b:208). In some creoles, it is *sa-(l)a* which may provide this contrast with *sa,* e.g., Dominican Creole (DC) *sa bèl, men sa-a lèd* 'this is pretty, but that is ugly' (Taylor 1951:46). In GC, Poyen-Bellisle (1894) records *sa* in proverbs and in animal tales, but presents *sila* and *sila-la,* glossed respectively 'celui-ci' and 'celui-là', in the grammatical section. The latter demonstrative is in competition with *tala,* according to Poyen-Bellisle. Goodman (1964:51f.) believes *sila* is now obsolete in GC, but that it originally meant 'this' in opposition to *sa* 'that'. Germain (1976:80) reports a more complex system for the demonstrative pronoun in GC: *sila* 'celui-ci' versus *sala* and *tala* 'celui-là', as well as *séla* 'ceux-ci, ceux-là'. There is also *lésèz,* glossed as 'ceux-là' and 'celle-là', and usually used in combination with *(lé)zòt.*[2] According to him, there are also "neuter" forms corresponding to French *ce, ça, ceci, cela.* Germain further includes the copula *sé* with the demonstrative pronouns (Valdman 1978b:233f.) as well as *mi* 'voici, voilà' (cf. Spanish *mirar*), which should probably be labeled 'présentatif' (Valdman 1978b:226).

Some of the above views are not specifically based on data for GC, but are rather attempts to give an overview of pronouns in French-based creoles. It is my belief that results of my 1978 fieldwork in Guadeloupe reveal data not yet covered in the literature and that they will call for revision of previous statements. To begin with, the demonstratives *sa, sila, tala, séla* do indeed exist as indicated by Germain. The pronoun *sa* is, of course, the unmarked demonstrative shared with all other French-based creoles. The use of *sila* and *tala* does not represent a proximity contrast, but rather one of emphasis. Given a sentence such as *an préféré sila ki tala* 'je préfère celui-ci à celui-là', Tessonneau (personal communication) states that "Les démonstratifs *sila* et *tala* ne sont pas différenciés comme 'this' et 'that'. C'est surtout leur contexte qui engendre *le choix de la traduction*" [italics mine]. During transcription and analysis, my Guadeloupean assistant felt that the basic contrast was *sila/séla,* i.e., singular versus plural, and that *tala* was used "pour insister." The distinctive features surely must be [+/– singular, +/– emphatic]. The system presented by Poyen-Bellisle (1894:40) is not totally incompatible with such a system although he opposes *sila* and *sila-la,* with the latter occurring less frequently than *tala.* He correctly points out the relationship of *tala* to the possessive pronoun which is formed by *ta* + pronoun or noun. This construction itself has the semantic effect of a demonstrative pronoun, e.g., *ta papa-a-ou-la* 'celui de ton père' (Germain 1976:80). As a matter of fact, Poyen-Bellisle may have incorrectly analyzed the relationship of *sila* to *sila-la.* In the textual material provided in the book, *sa* was more frequent than *sila-la,* and the latter may well be *sila* with a definite determiner.

As expected, my data show *sa* as a basic form of the demonstrative pronoun, and it may occur as subject (followed by *ki*), or as object. In this invariable form, it is functionally equivalent to French *ce, ceci, cela,* as well as to the members of the *celui, ceux* paradigms. Number, gender, animateness are unmarked. The following sentences are to be noted:

/1/ *ki-jan-sa ka maché*
'comment est-ce que ça marche?'

/2/ *mètrès-la kriyé non a sa ki té la*
'la maîtresse appela les noms de ceux qui étaient là (*Mòfwaz* 2:38)

/3/ *tou sa ki . . .*
'tous ceux qui . . .'

/4/ *a pa kon sa-on sa pasé*
'ce n'est pas comme ceci que ça s'est passé'[3]

/5/ *sa (k)i ka konté sé . . .*
'ce qui compte c'est . . .'

/6/ *sa an vlé sé on bon liv*
'ce que je veux c'est un bon livre'

/7/ *sé sa ou di la*
'c'est ce que tu as dit'
/8/ *kon sa i ka netwayé kò-a-i*
'comme ça il peut se nettoyer'

In some cases, *sa* may be expanded to mark animateness by the suffixation of *biten* or *moun:*

/9/ *gadé tou sa-biten yo ni a fè avan yo di you ka planté bannann*
'examiner toute chose qu'ils ont à faire avant de dire qu'ils plantent des bananes' (*Ja Ka Ta* 6:3)
/10/ *an ki-jan fè tou sa-moun pa la*
'comment se fait-il que cette quantité de personnes n'était pas là' (*Mòfwaz* 2:38)

The GC speaker uses *sila, séla* and sometimes *tala* primarily with reference to humans, but not entirely, for example:

/11/ *an ké vwé yo té ké planté séla*
'je verrai qu'ils pourraient planter ceux-là'
/12/ *an vwé sila*
'je vois celui-là'
/13/ *sé sila ki palé ban mwen*
'c'est celui qui m'a parlé'
/14/ *sé tala an té vwé*
'c'est celui que j'ai vu'

4. Relative Pronouns

With the exception of Indian Ocean creoles, the relative pronoun *ki* is expressed only when it is the subject of a relative clause (Goodman 1964:102). While zero morpheme for the object pronoun is typical of American creoles, *kè* sometimes occurs in what is probably a *créole francisé,* e.g., *lajan-la kè ou té pwété mwen-la* 'l'argent que vous m'avez prêté'. Salcède (1976:54) finds that *kè* is increasingly used as an object relative in creoles. The following sentences are typical:

/15/ *sa ki ka konté sé . . .*
'ce qui compte c'est . . .' (subject)
/16/ *sa an vlé sé on bon liv*
'ce que je veux c'est un bon livre' (object)

It should be pointed out that a more informal version of /15/ would involve consonantal deletion in *ki: sa-i ka konté sé . . .* (Germain 1976:82). Daniel Racine (personal communication) says that such a transformation would be blocked in certain environments, e.g., *si ni ki pa ka tann . . .* 's'il y en a qui n'entendent pas . . .' because such deletion would cause hiatus.

We have already noted the extension of the relativizer to the object slot. The language is evidently developing a complementizer for sentence complements. Germain (1976:83) points out that the interrogative pronouns *(ki-moun, ki-biten, ki-sa, ka)* are being shifted from their interrogative function to the function of complementizer for "phrases complétives" as well, e.g., *an koumansé konpwann ka jandab yé* 'je commence à comprendre ce que c'est qu'un gendarme', *mwen sa vwé ka sé-lézòt-la ja apwann* (*Mòfwaz* 2:35) 'je vois ce que les autres ont déjà appris', *an mandé-ou ki-moun-ki voyé-ou* 'je vous demande (celui) qui vous a envoyé'. It will be noted that these examples more closely resemble what Dubois and Dubois-Charlier (1970:244) refer to as "phrases relatives" rather than "complétives des syntagmes prépositionnels," i.e., a sentence such as *je me souviens de ce que vous m'avez dit* is equivalent to [*je me souviens de cela*$_S$ [*vous m'avez dit cela*]$_S$]. This deep structure analysis would not be valid for the creole example. There are examples in Poyen-Bellisle (1894) which show *sa* in what I believe to be a complementizer function, e.g., *sa zyé pa wé kè pa ka fè mal* 'ce que les yeux ne voient le coeur ne peut pas blesser', *epi mandé li sa i té ka fè la* 'et [le lapin] lui a demandé ce qu'il était en train de faire', *chak-moun sav sa ki ka bouyi* 'chacun sait ce qui est en train de bouillir'. Note that in examples /5/, /6/, and /7/ we have sentences in which *sa* is topicalized, and therefore these examples do not show *sa* in the complementizer function. In his discussion of the relative, Poyen-Bellisle (1894:40f.) indicates that creole still has *qui,* but has lost *que* and *lequel;* and he is of the opinion that these latter forms have been lost because of certain "combinaisons phonétiques par groupe" as seen in the sentence *sé i mwen ka wé* 'c'est lui que je vois' rather than **sé i ka mwen ka wé.*

5. Interrogative Pronouns

Goodman (1964:52f.) remarks that American creoles extend the use of *sa* from relative constructions to interrogative ones. He compares this usage to *what* in the English sentences *what he wants* and *what does he want,* where the difference is signaled by verbal syntax. French-based creoles may show no overt syntactic difference, e.g., Martinican Creole (MC) *sa ou ka pòté kon sa* 'que portes-tu comme ça?' or *sa* in early examples of indirect interrogation in GC: *epi mandé li sa i té ka fè la* 'et [le lapin] lui a demandé ce qu'il y faisait' (Poyen-Bellisle 1894:59); *Sept Heures mandé sa ki la* 'Sept Heures a demandé qui était là' (Parsons 1936:308). Interrogative *sa* may be differentiated, however, from the relative pronoun by preposing it with *ki,* and this pronoun may refer to persons as well as to things (Goodman 1964:52, n. 47). Germain (1976:83) gives an example for GC: *ki-sa ki pa fen, bon maten-la* 'qui n'a pas faim, ce matin?'[4] In general, however, GC uses *ka* rather than *sa* as an interrogative pronoun in reference to things. In addition to *ka,* GC has expanded the interrogative pronoun system by combining *ki* and the indefinite nouns *moun* 'personne' and *biten* 'chose', e.g., *ki-moun (ki)* 'qui' and *ki-biten (ki)* 'qu'est-ce qui'. Still another interrogative pronoun is *kilès (ki)* 'lequel', which, unlike *lequel* in French, seems to refer only to persons, although, like French, it has a partitive or restrictive sense. There is also a plural counterpart *ki-yo* 'lesquels' (Germain 1976:83). Note the following examples:

/17/ *ka ki tonbé la*
'qu'est-ce qui vient de tomber?'
/18/ *ka ou ka fè*
'qu'es-tu en train de faire?'
/19/ *ka sa yé*
'comment vas-tu?'
/20/ *ka i ni* 'qu'a-t-il?' versus *ka ki tini* 'qu'est-ce qu'il y a?'
/21/ *ki biten zòt tini la*
'qu'est-ce que vous avez là?'
/22/ *ta-ki-moun sé-ti-moun-la-sa*
'à qui sont ces enfants?'
/23/ *ki-moun ki vin, pon-moun*
'qui est venu? personne'
/24/ *kilès ki pli fò*
'lequel est plus fort?'
/25/ *pa kilès nou ka koumansé*
'par qui allons-nous commencer?'

One must account for time, place, and manner adverbials in this system. In this case, *ki* combines with nouns such as *tan* 'temps', *jan* 'genre, manière', *koté* 'côté, endroit'.

/26/ *i mandé-i ki-tan i ni lentansyon fin koupé pyé-bwa-la*
'il lui a demandé quand il avait l'intention de finir de couper l'arbre'
/27/ *ki-jan sa ka maché*
'comment est-ce que ça marche?'
/28/ *yo sé moun ki-koté*
'ils sont des gens de quel pays?'

The adverbials *oti, ola,* and *o* compete with *ki-koté* in a sentence such as *ola ou té yé* 'où étais-tu?', although *ki-koté* in /28/ occurs in a unique context (point of origin). The forms for *pourquoi* should be mentioned: *pou ki-biten, pou ki-sa,* and *poukwa.*

6. Indefinite Pronouns

Germain (1976:85) claims that creole indefinite pronouns do not show an increase in referential power beyond that seen in those of French. This claim seems to be supported when we list certain creolized forms of French indefinites, e.g., *pèsonn* 'personne', *dòt* 'd'autres', *séten* 'certains', *tròp* 'trop', *plizyè* 'plusieurs', *asé* 'assez', *pé* 'peu', *menm* 'même', *ayen* 'rien', *kyèkzen* 'quelques-uns', *onpil* 'une pile, beaucoup', *tout* 'tout', *konmen* 'combien', and others. The truth of the matter is that GC has developed a derivational matrix for indefinite concepts (see Figure 1, below). Basic to such a matrix are the nouns *moun, biten, koté, tan, jan,* and the like. There are, of course, several *cases vides,* but the potential is present for structural expansion.

	moun	biten	koté	tan	jan	sa	yonn	gout	bwen
∅	+	+	+	+	+	+	+	+	+
on	+	+	+						
tout	+	+		+					
ki	+	+	+			+			
pon	+		+		+		+		
ti	+	+						+	+
gran	+								
chak	+	+	+						
nenpòt-ki	+	+	+		+				
lézòt	+								
(on)dòt	+	+	+						
menm		+							
bèl		+							
mal		+							

Figure 1
Derivational Matrix

All these forms may occur in a generic sense in a noun phrase, e.g., *on sèl biten* 'une seule chose', *sé-moun-la* 'les gens', *pa lòt koté-a-kaz-la* 'de l'autre côté de la maison', *koté-la nou k ay la tou pré* 'l'endroit où nous allons est tout près', *palé biten antanlontan* 'parler des choses d'antan'. In combination with derivational prefixes, words like *moun, biten,* and *koté* become complex lexemes (Conklin 1962; Pottier 1970) and may remain functionally a noun, or they become a pronoun or an adverb insofar as the French equivalent is concerned, as we see in the following lists:

moun 'generic'	*biten* 'generic'	*koté* 'generic, prep.'
on moun 'q'n'	*on biten* 'q'chose'	*on koté* 'q'part'
ki-moun 'qui'	*ki-biten* 'qu'est-ce qui'	*ki-koté* 'où'
ti-moun 'enfant'	*menm-biten* 'semblable'	*dòt-koté* 'd'autre part'
gran-moun 'adulte'	*tout biten* 'tout'	
tout moun 'tous'		
chak moun 'chacun'		

The fact that we are dealing with complex lexemes can be seen in the syntactic behavior of certain derivations in combination with noun determiners, e.g., *on biten* 'q'chose', *on dòt-biten ankò* 'autre chose encore'; *sé-ti-moun-la menm-biten* 'les enfants sont semblables', *dé menm-biten* 'deux [enfants] semblables'; *sé-moun-la* 'les gens', *sé-ti-moun-la* 'les enfants', *sé-lezòt-ti-moun-an-mwen-la* 'mes autres enfants'. However, a part of the matrix, the indefinite adjectives *tou(t)* and *chak,* behaves differently in the syntax, e.g., *tout-moun* 'tous' beside *tou sé-ti-moun-la* 'tous les enfants', *chak-moun* 'chacun' beside *chak sé-ti-moun-la* 'chacun des enfants'.

Among negatives, we must cite *ayen* and *hak,* both meaning 'rien', or those formed with *pon* 'aucun', which I derive from *pa* 'neg.' and *on* 'un'. The resulting *pon* combines with nouns or pronouns to form negative pronouns, e.g., *moun* 'personne' (non-neg.)/*pon-moun* 'personne' (neg.), *yonn* 'l'un'/*pon-yonn* 'pas un seul', *koté* 'côté, endroit'/*pon-koté* 'nulle part', *jan* 'genre, manière'/*an pon-jan* 'en aucune manière'.

7. Conclusions

In their search for clues to the genesis and development of creoles, scholars have generally agreed on the affinities between French-based creoles and overseas or popular French. The conception of Chaudenson (1973:370) is that creoles and French constitute a kind of "continuum" cutting across geography and across history and that the same linguistic system has been transformed in many different ways due to a diversity of sociocultural structures and contact situations. We cannot deny this common base, and this fact is evident in the pronominal subsystems, as presented in Figure 2, p. 99, and Figure 3, p. 100.

	GC	LA	LC	LT	SE
1	an, mwen	mwen	mo, mwen	mo, mwen	mo, mwa
2	(v)ou	to, twé	to, twa	to, twa	ou
3	(l)i	(l)i	li	li	(l)i
4	nou	nou	nou(zòt)	nou(zòt)	nou
5	zòt	ou, zòt	vou(zòt)	(v)ou(zòt)	zot
6	yo	yo	yé	yé	zot

Abbreviations: GC (Guadeloupean Creole), LA (Lesser Antillean), LC (Louisiana Creole), LT (Louisiana Tales), SE (Seychellois)

Figure 2
Personal Pronouns

Here I have assembled partial data from five creole dialects: Guadeloupean Creole (Morgan 1979 and field notes); early Lesser Antillean (Marbot 1869, Poyen-Bellisle 1894); Louisiana Creole (Lane 1935, Morgan 1969 and field notes); Louisiana Folktales (Brueyre 1878, Mercier 1880, Fortier 1895); and Seychellois (Bollée 1977). Valdman (1978a:50) distinguishes two groups of creole dialects. The first (Indian Ocean, Louisiana, and French Guyana) is labeled conservative and is characterized by the pre-position of the demonstrative and possessive determiners. He considers pre-position to be typical of, say, "créole de salon" as spoken by colonial whites in Santo Domingo. This conservative group is contrasted with an innovative group favoring post-position of determiners, which reached its greatest development in Haiti. This innovation suggests a substratum source on the basis of patterns in West African languages and in pidginized popular French of Abidjan. The group of five dialects (represented in Figures 2 and 3) includes two from the conservative group, Louisiana, and a representative dialect of the Indian Ocean. It should be noted that whereas Lesser Antillean is placed with the innovative group, it differs from the other dialects with respect to the pre-posed plural marker. For the sake of gaining perspective, I have consulted earlier texts for both Lesser Antillean and for Louisiana.

In his discussion of morphology, Poyen-Bellisle (1894:38-41) gives clues to the status of LA creole grammar in the 19th century. He labels certain morphemes and constructions as learned, as opposed to others which he classifies as true creole. In the case of indefinite pronouns, Poyen-Bellisle states that the only ones are

	GC	LA	LC	LT	SE
Demonstrative	sa, sila(tala)	sa, sila/sila-la	sa, sila	sa, sila	sa-(la), sa-mem
	séla	(tala)			
Relative	sa, ka, N+(ki)	N+(ki)	N+ki/kè, sèski	N+ki	ki-(sa)
Interrogative	(pou)ki+N	(ki)+N	ki, sèski	(ki)-sa	ki, kwa
	(pou)(ki)+sa	poukwò	kèski	kofè	ki-sen-la
	kilès	kilès	manyèr, koman	koman	ki-manyer
		kan	kan	kan, tan	kot
		konben	ou	ki-tan	
		kouman			
Indefinite	moun	moun	moun, léjan	moun	dimoun
	on moun	pesonn	dumonn		en dimoun
	pon-moun	chak-moun	kèkenn	kèkenn	kekdimoun
			kèkzèn	chaken	saken
			chaken		
	biten	kichoz	kèkchòz	kichòj, buten	kèksoz
	ayen	anyen	aryen	a(r)yen	naryen
	koté	koté	kèkpar	kèkpar	
	pon-koté		nulpar		
	on koté				

Figure 3
Demonstrative, Relative, Interrogative, and Indefinite Pronouns

tout, pesonn, chak, oken, plizyè, which he classifies as learned, beside *toupilen* 'tout plein' and *anpil,* which are creole. He must have listed the only indefinite pronouns current in his speech, for a search of textual material in his book reveals pronouns not discussed in the morphology section, e.g., *chak-moun, tout-moun, tout-ki-choz, tibwen, sa-menm, tout-sa, anyen, ak* 'rien', *konman, kilès.* His labeling of morphemes as either learned or creole suggests that there existed a "créole de salon" current among members of the planter class. This variety of creole was in contrast with the "créole sec" found in the tale of *konpè lapen e konpè zanba* dictated to him by an elderly black. We have similar evidence of this in Louisiana. Larocque-Tinker (1956:100ff.) tells us that throughout the 19th century creole was in vogue as a literary language among whites, and I believe it was this period of literary and scholarly production by bilingual whites that exerted the greatest influence on LC norms. In LC data we find evidence of a kind of "relexification" of creole structures. In Fortier (1895) there are constructions such as *kichoj, tou-kichoj, tou-ki-dòt-choj,* which are matched by Saint Martin: *kèk-chòz, tou-kèk-chòz, tou-kèk-dòt-chòz.* Post-creole restructuring is also evident in the syntax, e.g., the development of a subject-object contrast in relative pronouns in sentences such as *sa fè dèlapen ki mòr* 'ça fait deux lapin qui sont morts' versus *chòz kè mo tè lèmen* 'une chose que j'aimais'.

Unlike LC, GC has reversed the trend of "créole de salon." Even if this dialect were, for the most part, going its own way, there is still some evidence for both superstrate and substrate input. First of all, creolized forms such as *pèsonn, tròp, asè,* and the like, still represent French form and content. In the derivational matrix, the expansion of paradigmatic classes with *moun, biten, koté* and others also continues this French presence, albeit in a more regular and more symmetrical way. We have only to search regional dictionaries to find in New World French and in Western and Central France words like *monde* 'les gens', *le grand-monde* 'les adultes', *le petit-monde* 'les enfants', which reflect the semantic features of GC *moun, gran-moun,* and *ti-moun.* The same is possible for regional French *butin* and *ça* (Glossaire s.v. *monde, butin;* Poirier 1953 s.v. *monde, ça*). Conversely, I find interesting the morphosyntax for relative and interrogative pronouns typical of West African languages, e.g., Ewé *amé* 'homme' + *ka* 'quel' → *améka* 'qui', *nú* 'chose' + *ka* 'quelle' → *núka* 'quelle chose', *afí* 'endroit' + *ka* 'quel' → *afíka* 'où' (Westermann 1942-43). Of course post-position is privileged in Ewé. GC has post-position for most noun determiners, but has pre-position in the derivational matrix (Figure 3, p. 106). The matrix involves semantic modification, i.e., *moun* 'generic' becomes *tout-moun* 'tous', *ki-moun* 'qui', *pon-moun* 'personne (neg.)', *ti-moun* 'enfant', and the like.

Poyen-Bellisle (1894:38) claims that there is no gender or number distinction in LA although number may sometimes be indicated by the demonstrative adjective *ces,* e.g., *nonm-la, sé-nonm-la.* A search through the animal tale, proverbs, and *énigmes* in the Poyen-Bellisle volume does indeed show this to be true. Count nouns without determiners could be interpreted as generic, i.e., a class term for the totality of the species, e.g., *pyé-bwa tini zowèy* 'les arbres ont des oreilles'; or, a noun would occur with a numeral or with an adjective such as *tout, anpil: tout ti-kichoz* 'toutes les petites choses', *anpil piti piti-la* 'beaucoup d'enfants', *kat boutèy pilen lèt* 'quatre bouteilles pleines de lait'. By contrast *yonn* 'un' would specify singular, e.g., *pa yonn moun* 'pas une seule personne'. LA seems to have been a creole in search of a plural determiner. The remark by Poyen-Bellisle that number was sometimes indicated by the demonstrative adjective suggests that a change was in progress at a late stage of development. The demonstrative determiner function had been preempted by French dialectal *sila,* which had the role of both a pronoun and an adjective (Glossaire s.v. *cui-là*), and the dialect had recourse only to the French plural demonstrative adjective for the new plural determiner function. This form was also given the function of plural demonstrative pronoun. At this point, the reader will be reminded of the plural determiner *lésèz,* which occurred in the context *lésèz adan zòt* 'ceux parmi vous' (Germain 1976:81). This pronoun has been replaced by *séla.* D. Racine (personal communication) considers *lésèz* to be very rare, perhaps even *archaic* [italics mine]. He would use it rather in a context meant to be amusing or pedantic. Normally he would say *sa-i adan zòt, moun adan zòt,* or *séla adan zòt.* In another case of morphosyntactic change, GC seems to be in the process of adding a *ki/kè* opposition in relative clauses. It is reported that there is fluctuation between zero morpheme and *kè* in the object function (Salcède 1976:54). This change has already been completed in LC. In GC the change would seem to be evidence of restructuring at the post-creole stage, and this conclusion seems valid due to the fact that *kè* is an imported form. On the other hand, I think that the shift of *ka* as an interrogative pronoun to a new function as a complementizer is more typical of the developmental stage.

NOTES

1. Data are based on recorded speech as well as written texts. Sources for written materials include: Germain 1976; the monthly magazine, *Ja Ka Ta;* and the review, *Mòfwaz.* Sentences, originally transcribed in phonemics, were later rewritten in the orthographic system of GEREC, CUAG, see Bernabé 1977. My fieldwork in Guadeloupe was funded by the Rackham School of Graduate Studies, The University of Michigan. All recordings were transcribed and edited with the aid of Mlle. Catherine Vercautrin of Abymes. Her valuable assistance is hereby

acknowledged. In addition, I wish to thank Professor Daniel Racine, Howard University, and Mlle. Louise Tessonneau, CNRS, Paris, for their extremely important comments.

2. Glossaire s.v. *ceuses,* Clapin s.v. *ceuz: les ceuz qui voudront v'nir avec nous autes.* In addition to these examples for Québec, *les ceuz* is found in the popular speech of Western and Central France, Louisiana, and Acadie (Brunot and Bruneau 1949; Phillips 1978:177; Poirier 1953 s.v. *ceux, ceuses*).

3. In /4/ the *-on* suffix in *sa-on* is an interesting case of what my *assistante* termed "une particule enjoliveuse." It appears in negative sentences; a second example is *a pa jé-on* 'il n'y avait pas de jeux'. Westermann (1942:18, 21, 26) gives the following examples of negative sentences in Ewé: *mewòna* 'je fais', but *nye méwòna-o* 'je ne fais pas', *ménye Kofi-o* 'ce n'est pas Kofi', *yi* 'va', but *me ga yi-o* 'ne va pas'.

4. Goodman (1964:52f.) suggests *quoi* as the source of *ka,* but points out the possibility of either a Carib or African source. See also Taylor 1951:46.

IDENTIFYING THE AFRICAN GRAMMATICAL BASE OF THE CARIBBEAN CREOLES: A Typological Approach

Martha M. Baudet
University of Pittsburgh

Studies concerned with the grammatical influence of African languages on the Caribbean creoles (e.g., Sylvain 1936; Taylor 1963; Goodman 1964; Hall 1966) have failed to determine precisely the role of African languages in the formation of these creoles. While investigations have collected considerable evidence for Africanisms in the creoles, many have placed more emphasis on finding European grammatical sources, and none have included a systematic typological analysis of relevant African languages. This article argues for the necessity of using a typological approach in the search for the origins of these creoles and presents some results of a preliminary investigation along these lines. The comparison of primary data from Ewe, Yoruba, Igbo, Twi, Haitian Creole, and Jamaican Creole reveals many typologically marked syntactic parallels between the creoles and all four West African languages. The results support the hypothesis that the Caribbean creoles' chief grammatical structures are those common to the various West Afrian input languages, and further typological analysis of the likely African sources is encouraged.[1]

1. Motivation for the Study

Most creolists agree that African languages have had some influence on the formation of the Caribbean creoles, but the extent and precise sources of the African influence are unresolved matters. While various studies have given evidence for phonological, syntactic, semantic, and some lexical correspondences between the two language groups, I am restricting myself in this paper to the problem of establishing the syntactic sources of these creoles.

Since creoles have often been considered to be genetically related to their vocabulary source languages, many attempts to identify the linguistic origins of the Caribbean creoles have emphasized the similarities between European and creole structures. Although such accounts are based largely on lexical comparisons, linguists adhering to standard historical methodology have sought to establish syntactic correspondences as well. But since syntactic parallels are mostly limited to typologically unmarked structures and patterns that seem to appear universally in creoles, evidence for such syntactic relatedness is weak. Hall (1966:86), for example, argues that the syntax of creoles consists of " 'reduced structures' resulting from the intentional simplification of European languages by their speakers when conversing with supposedly childish natives [Africans]." Hall further attempts to explain the fact that Caribbean creoles with different vocabulary bases manifest striking syntactic parallels. Although he recognizes the appearance of certain West African patterns in the creoles, he would account for the similarities among them primarily by the fact that the same strategies of simplification were used by the different European groups. His theory assumes that the creoles are expanded pidgins that sprang up wherever the need for communication arose between Europeans and Africans (1966:20).

Valdman (1971, 1975) and Chaudenson (1973) have sought to strengthen the argument that much of French creole grammatical structure finds its roots in French by looking for additional parallels in non-standard French dialects that might have been at the scene of creolization in the Caribbean.[2] More recently, Valdman (1976b:133) argues that the appearance of African features in the Caribbean creoles was a gradual process resulting from the restructuring of the target language by the substrate speakers. He believes that the early stages of the Caribbean creoles show great variation, and using Whinnom's (1971) terminology, he likens their development to secondary hybrids that gradually evolved into tertiary hybrids. Valdman's evidence for the degree of early variation that he assumes is, however, drawn from sources that one would expect to be heavily Gallicized,[3] and he himself admits that intermediate stages are not attested (1976b:117-18).

Other creolists, such as Taylor (1963, 1977), Goodman (1964), and Hull (1975), feel that an Afro-Portuguese pidgin or creole is the only logical source that could satisfactorily explain the African features recurring throughout the Caribbean. Whinnom (1971), adopting the Sabir theory (cf. Thompson 1961), would further maintain that all creole languages in the world are relexifications of the Lingua Franca of the Mediterranean that arose during the Crusades. Allsopp (1976:18) also claims to support the monogenesis hypothesis although he argues that the Africans directly calqued their native language patterns in the various European vocabulary source languages.

If the Caribbean creoles originated as a relexified Afro-Portuguese pidgin, this would explain the extensive African grammatical input. However, there is no strong historical evidence for any pidgin stage; furthermore, as Alleyne (1971:175) points out, the contact situation between the Europeans and the slave trading centers did not call for the invention of a trade jargon:

> It was rather a question of two types of communities in contact without serious attempts at social integration, and of one type, African, seeing it in their interests to learn the language of the other type of community (European).

Although it is fragmentary, historical documentation of the slave trade at the time of the colonization of the Caribbean indicates that the slaves came from diverse linguistic backgrounds. Herskovits (1958) and LePage (1960), for example, both report, on the basis of available documents, that the gathering of slaves took place over a vast area extending from Senegal to Angola. Although in general the traders conducted business at the coastal ports, the slaves themselves almost always came from the interior; the coastal tribesmen acted in cooperation with the traders, and in exchange for European goods, they provided them with prisoners from tribal wars that were occurring frequently with all neighbors and often extended far inland. Not only did the totality of the slave operations reach a vast area, but also any particular group of slaves leaving for the New World was sure to be linguistically heterogeneous because the dealers intentionally mixed them to make communication, and hence insurrection, unlikely.

Historical documentation does not exclude the possibility that some slaves could have learned a Portuguese pidgin, yet we have no actual reports of such a pidgin being spoken by the slaves going to the New World. Furthermore, there is no need to assume direct Portuguese pidgin influence if we can adequately account for the development of the Caribbean creoles without making such a strong assumption.[4]

Sylvain (1936:178) considered African grammatical input into Caribbean creoles to be so striking that she classified Haitian Creole (HC) as an African language:

> Nous sommes en présence d'un français coulé dans le moule de la syntaxe africaine ou, comme on classe généralement les langues d'après leur parenté syntaxique, d'une langue Ewé à vocabulaire français.[5]

Aside from her misconception of historical linguistic methodology, Sylvain's choice of Ewe as Haitian Creole's grammar source does not even account for her own evidence. Since she has found structural parallels among a number of West African languages and Haitian Creole, the only reason she seems to have for choosing one particular African language is that her primary data are restricted to Ewe while her other Africa examples come from secondary sources. She fails, furthermore, to notice many marked grammatical parallels, no doubt in part because she considers African linguistic structure to be "very simple" (1936:36).[6] But more importantly, in choosing one language as Haitian Creole's grammatical source, Sylvain has overlooked a crucial methodological requirement for this type of investigation: the need for a typological comparison of the various languages that might have provided grammatical input with the creoles themselves. As a result, her analysis had no theoretical framework that would have allowed her to give a satisfactory evaluation of her data.

The lack of conclusive evidence for a pidgin stage in the development of the Caribbean creoles, together with our knowledge of the contact situation, seems to have important implications for an adequate theory of their formation. Thomason and Kaufman (1975:21-22) emphasize the fact that the Africans were not socially integrated into the European community and argue that their attempt to shift to the European language would have produced an unsuccessful acquisition of the grammatical structures of the target language. Furthermore, they (1975:23-24) argue that in this situation one would expect to find "a combination of shared marked grammatical features and (perhaps unshared) unmarked ones from those languages which contributed to the grammar," namely, West African languages. This hypothesis would also explain the recurring grammatical parallels throughout the Caribbean since the creoles arose under similar circumstances and involved typologically similar African languages.

Thomason and Kaufman (1975:19) even suggest that the Africans acquired "only the TL vocabulary, but not the TL phonology, morphology, or syntax," a case which they term "abrupt creolization." My findings indicate that although we cannot attribute *all* syntactic input to West African languages (or at least that European languages had a strong influence on the choice of some African patterns over others), the historical and linguistic evidence supports the hypothesis that the Africans' shift to the superstrate languages was abrupt and would encourage us to look not at one, but at a variety, of the typologically similar West African languages for the source of the syntactic structures of the creoles.

Although intermittent allusions to Africanisms in creoles have been found in the literature ever since Sylvain's attempt to establish Haitian Creole as a daughter of Ewe, no one, to my knowledge, has made a systematic analysis of primary data from a large number of West African languages in an attempt to see if the grammar of the creoles represents a "lowest common denominator" of these suspected sources. One reason is perhaps that the assumptions motivating this direction of research seem to contradict traditional beliefs about historical language development; such an investigation forces us to abandon the hypothesis that the chief grammatical ties of the creoles are to their European source languages. At the same time, since most of the creoles' vocabulary comes from the European languages, no one (except Sylvain) would want to claim genetic affiliation to one or more African languages. Thomason and Kaufman (1975:24) reason that "a language . . . that derives its vocabulary from one source and its grammar from some other(s) is not genetically related to any of its source languages." I agree with their conclusion that languages such as the Caribbean creoles, with different lexical and grammatical sources, are not instances of normal transmission and hence should not be considered to be related to any of their sources in the normal genetic sense.

The investigation described in the remainder of this paper is preliminary in the sense that it deals with primary data drawn from only two Caribbean creoles and four West African languages. I hope, however, that it will serve as a pilot study for more comprehensive African-creole comparisons that will eventually resolve the issue of the grammatical origins of the Caribbean creoles.

2. Research Method

After examining Caribbean creole texts and secondary sources to identify constructions that seem to be of non-European origin, I checked these constructions against West African languages of Greenberg's Niger-Congo group (including West Atlantic, Mande, Voltaic, and Kwa subgroups) which are spoken in the part of West Africa from which most of the slaves were taken, i.e., the area comprising the modern countries of Senegal, Gambia, Sierra Leone, Liberia, Ghana, Togoland, Benin, and Nigeria (Greenberg 1966:177). I noted grammatical structures that paralleled those of the creoles and then compiled a 199-item questionnaire in English that I hoped would elicit the patterns common to the typologically similar Niger-Congo languages and the Caribbean creoles. Next, I ran my questionnaire on native speakers (one for each language) of Haitian Creole, Jamaican Creole, Ewe, Yoruba, Igbo, and Twi. The four West African languages are among those frequently mentioned as the most probable native languages of the slaves taken to Haiti and Jamaica.

3. Results

Below I present the grammatical features which I found to be particularly indicative of a West African substratum in the Caribbean creoles. Examples drawn from secondary sources as well as primary data include: the structure and word order of determiners and nominalizers; genitives; comparative constructions; serial verbs; distributive constructions; and coordinators.[7]

3.1. Determiners and nominalizers: structure and word order

Determiners and nominalizers follow the elements they modify in Haitian Creole, Ewe, Yoruba, Igbo, Kpelle, and Twi. When both a demonstrative and the definite article are present, the demonstrative comes first, as in the following examples:

/1a/ H: kay-sa-a
house-that-DET
'that house' (V315)

/1b/ E: afe-a
house-that

/1c/ Y: ile yen
house that
/1d/ I: ụnọ afu
house that
/1e/ K: pérɛi tî
house that (W286)
/1f/ H: moun-sila-yo
people-this-PL
'these people'
/1g/ E: ame-sia-wo
people-this-PL
/1h/ T: abofrá yi
child this
'this child' (C49)

Taylor (1971:295) indicates that postposed demonstratives are also characteristic of Louisiana, Lesser Antillean, Sranan, Saramaccan, Papiamentu, and Gulf of Guinea creoles.

In Haitian Creole, any non-nominal element can be nominalized by the suffixation of the definite article:

/2a/ H: plaf-plaf-la
plop-plop-DET
'the plop-plopping' (H60)
/2b/ H: pâdâ m-malad-la
during I-sick-DET
'during the time I was sick' (H60)

The determiner also follows relative clauses in Haitian Creole as well as in Ewe:

/2c/ H: oto li van-mouen an
car he sell-me DET
'the car which he sold me' (V32)
/2d/ E: evu si wòdzra nam la
vehicle which he-sold to-me DET

And Twi uses a special particle *no* to mark both nominalized clauses and relatives. (In /2e/ below, *na* anticipates the subject.)

/2e/ T: aberra na meyara no
time ANT I-sick NOM
'during the time I was sick'

/2f/ T: nantwie a wo tɔnee maa wo nua no
cow that you sell-PAST to your brother NOM
'the cow you sold to your brother'

In Yoruba, an entire sentence can be topicalized by adding *ni* at the end:

/2g/ Y: ó ra ewúrẹ́ ni
he buy goat TOP
'the point is that he bought a goat' (W313)

3.2. Genitives: structure and word order

Just as determiners follow their heads in many Caribbean creoles and West African languages, genitives, too, are often postposed. I found the same word order in Haitian Creole, Yoruba, and Igbo. In Ewe, only the possessive adjective is postposed, and in fact, this is true only for the first and second person singular adjectives and when the head is a kinship term or 'friend'.

/3a/ H: mâmâ ti-kouzê mwê
mother little-cousin my
'my little cousin's mother' (H48)

/3b/ Y: lya ọrẹ mi
mother friend my
'my friend's mother'

/3c/ I: nne eyi m
mother friend my

/3d/ E: xɔnye dada
friend-my mother

A more striking parallel exists among these languages in their formation of pronominal possessives. In each case the pronominal marker is suffixed to a word meaning 'property' or 'possession':

/4a/ H: pa-m
property-my
'mine' (H48)

/4b/ E: tɔnye
property-my

/4c/ Y: temi
possession-my
/4d/ I: nke-m
possession-my

3.3 Comparative constructions

Another remarkable similarity among the creoles and West African languages is the use of the verb meaning 'surpass' to form the comparative:

/5a/ H: piti pasé mwê
small surpass me
'smaller than I' (H52)
/5b/ E: sesẽ wum
strong surpass-me
'stronger than I'
/5c/ Y: loye ju mi lọ
intelligent surpass (ju . . . lọ) me
'more intelligent than I'
/5d/ I: wenalilu m ike
surpass me strength
'stronger than I'
/5e/ T: ketwa sene me
small surpass me
'smaller than I'

Hall (1966:82) notes that virtually all pidgins and creoles with an African substratum use this means of comparison. Among his examples are the following:

/5f/ Dahomean Pidgin English:
fine pass all woman
'finer than all (other) women'
/5g/ Gullah:
tɒl pas mi
'taller than I'
/5h/ Martinican Creole:
grã pase fi mwẽ
'older than my girl'
/5i/ Sranan:
pasá tén lítri
'more than ten liters'

3.4. Serial verbs

Both Caribbean creoles and West African languages have numerous verb sequences with no intervening connecting elements. While this feature in itself is characteristic of many non-creole languages, one particular verb sequence is notably similar in these two groups. This is the use of the verb meaning 'give' to indicate the direction or benefit of the first verb. In Haitian Creole, the verb 'give' is *ba(j):*

/6a/ H: pòt veso bã-m tire bèf-la ba u
bring vessel give-me milk cow-the give you
'bring a vessel for me to milk the cow for you (H(66)78)

Hall notes that *ba(j)* must be treated as a verb and not simply as a preposition because it takes the inflectional aspect prefixes, as in the following examples:

/6b/ H: m-a-ba u jũ kal
I-FUT-give you a beating
'I'll give you a beating' (H(66)79)

The following examples show the same construction in Ewe, Yoruba, Twi, and Efik:

/6c/ E: meɖa nu na wò
I-cook food give you
'I cook food for you'
/6d/ Y: ngo ṣe onjẹ alẹ fun ọ
I-FUT make food evening
'I will make dinner for you'
/6e/ T: mɘ noa aduane mawo
I cook food give-you
'I cook food for you'
/6f/ Ef: ánàm útóm ɔ́nɔ̀ mî
he-is-doing work he-give me
'he's working for me' (W371)

Other New World creoles also share this construction. Compare, for example, Gullah:

/6g/ G: dɛm də ca əm ɟi dɪ ɲɒɲ pipl
'they carry it to (lit. give) the young people' (H(66)79)

Taylor (1971:294-95) adds to the list Louisiana, Lesser Antillean, Cayenne, Jamaican, Sranan, Saramaccan, Negerhollands, and Gulf of Guinea creoles, suggesting that the verb 'give' functions as a dative preposition throughout the Caribbean creoles he has analyzed.

3.5. Distributive constructions

West African languages and Caribbean creoles show great resemblance in the following distributive construction:

/7a/ H: yo vini dis dis
they came ten ten
'they came ten by ten'
/7b/ J: dem come ten ten
they come ten ten
/7c/ E: wova ewo ewo
they-came ten ten
/7d/ T: ɔnom baa du du
they come-PAST ten ten
/7e/ Y: nwọn wa ni mẹwa mẹwa
they came by ten ten

The Ewe and Twi formations are identical to those of the creoles, and Yoruba is also similar.

3.6. Coordinators

Coordinating words in Haitian and Papiamentu are *ak* and *cu,* respectively, used between substantives, and *é* (Haitian) or *i* (Papiamentu), used elsewhere (between adjectives, sentences, etc.). While the probable derivation of *ak* is from French *avec*, and *cu* is from Spanish *con* 'with', their uses are not the same in the creoles. French *et* and Spanish *y* are coordinators meaning 'and', while *avec* and *con* are used in the sense of 'with' or 'accompanying'. West African languages, like the creoles, have different coordinators to connect different form classes. As the following examples show, the African language forms *ati* (Y), *kple* (E), *na* (I) connect nouns, while *tun* (Y), *ga le* (E), *n'* (I) connect other parts of speech:

/8a/ P: John cu María
John and Maria
'John and Maria' (G28)
/8b/ H: mâmâ-m ak papa-m
mother-my and father-my
'my mother and my father' (H44)

/8c/ Y: lya mi ati baba mi
mother my and father my
/8d/ E: danye kple fofonye
mother-my and father-my
/8e/ I: nnnem na nnam
mother-my and father-my

/9a/ P: cora, blancu i blou
red white and blue
'red, white, and blue' (G36)
/9b/ H: grâ e-gro
big and-fat
'big and fat' (H44)
/9c/ Y: o tobi o tun sanra
he big he and (= furthermore) fat
/9d/ E: mumu ga le legbee
green furthermore long
'green and long'
/9e/ I: nnukwu n'ibu
big and-fat
'big and fat'

4. Discussion

The features presented in Section 3 are among the most persuasive results of this study for several reasons. First, most of them are present in all the West African languages that were examined, as well as in most of the Caribbean creoles. Second, they have not been claimed to be features characteristic of creoles in general, except for those with African input; that is, no one has attributed their appearance to universal strategies of pidgin/creole formation. Third, since the features are not especially common in languages of the world in general, it is not likely that they would have appeared in the creoles independently of African influence.

The data presented here in fact reveal many additional syntactic parallels that are not as conclusive for one or more of the following reasons:[8]

1) They were not found in all four West African languages.
2) They are thought to be found in (pidgins and) creoles in general.
3) They appear fairly frequently in languages of the world.

At the same time, it is felt that these further similarities, particularly as they are so numerous, lend considerable support to the stronger evidence. Furthermore, study of other African languages would very likely show that at least some of these constructions are more widespread in Africa than the evidence here might suggest.

Those features that one might want to attribute to universal creole grammar rather than to an African substratum include: the extensive use of reduplication; the lack of true subordinators; and the use of the same word for different form classes without any derivational indication of the change in class. Another feature often proposed as a candidate for universal creole grammar—the tendency for verbal qualifiers to occur exterior to the predicate, having the whole predicate as their scope (Kay and Sankoff 1974:64; Bickerton 1974:8)—does not appear consistently in the West African data although it does apply to the creoles. In Ewe, for example, progressive and intentional markers occur after the verb, and in Igbo, the completed marker is post-verbal. Some verbal qualifiers, however, do occur before the verbs in all the African languages examined in this paper.

Additional parallels shown in the data comprising features that are widespread in languages in general include: the omission of the subordinator in object relatives; the use of the word meaning 'body' in reflexive constructions; a lack of connecting elements in many noun and verb sequences; and special equational, locative, and interrogative linking verbs.

5. Conclusions

The results of this study show that there is considerable similarity in syntactic patterns between the Caribbean creoles and West African languages, and substantial support is given to the hypothesis that creoles should be expected to exhibit those grammatical features common to all languages that provided grammatical input—which may include the vocabulary-source languages though not, perhaps, to a great extent in the Caribbean cases.

Many of the syntactic similarities examined here were not only found in all four West African languages but were also significantly different from corresponding standard English and French patterns. The force of this evidence is further strengthened by the fact that these properties seem, for the most part, to be uncommon both in languages of the world and in other pidgins and creoles; that is, they cannot be accounted for in terms of either typological language universals or universal creole strategies.

While a number of the findings presented in this paper are confirmed by similarities in other West African languages reported by secondary sources, additional parallel structures that have been found in only one language other than the creoles particularly point to the need for a more detailed typological analysis of many more West African languages. Similarly, while some information was available to me on other Caribbean creoles, further research should also attempt to examine more creoles in conjunction with African data. And, of course, the typological comparison should be expanded to include phonological, morphological, and lexical (including lexical semantic) subsystems of the languages.

When strategies of pidgin learning are better understood and when a more comprehensive account has been given of features common to all creoles, then we will be better able to isolate those parallels that should be discounted as merely coincidental with universal creole features. Additional research (such as that of Chaudenson 1973; Hull 1975; and Valdman 1971, 1975) on European dialects at the time of, and connected with, the colonization of the Caribbean will allow a more comprehensive evaluation of the extent of grammatical influence from the vocabulary base languages.[9]

Nevertheless, it is suggested that even the most tentative results of this study—similarities found also in a number of non-African, non-contact languages and similarities with parallels in French or English as well as West African languages—should not be discounted. Certain features may not be especially marked typologically, but if they can be found to characterize all, or the majority of, the West African languages involved and the creoles, their existence at least further validates the less ambiguous evidence. And if most of the European grammatical structures in the creoles also have West African analogues, this would suggest African influence on the choice of those European grammatical features that do appear in the creoles.

In essence, I feel that a significant portion of the findings of this study strongly supports the case for an African substratum in the Caribbean creoles. At the same time, these findings encourage future research in the directions that have been suggested as a promising approach to further clarification of the linguistic origins of the Caribbean creoles.

NOTES

1. I would like to thank Sarah G. Thomason of the University of Pittsburgh for reading and commenting on earlier drafts of this paper and for many helpful discussions and suggestions. I am also grateful to my informants: Adu Amankwaa, Florence Didigu, Winston Lawson, Emilia Obianim, Silas Ogunwande, and Léon Pamphile.

2. I do not mean to reject Hall's evidence for simplified structures in creole (cf. Ferguson 1971), or Valdman's or Chaudenson's evidence for parallels between the creoles and non-standard French dialects. My contention with such studies is merely that they undermine the significance of what I feel to be more obvious

sources of creole structure: both the linguistic data and our knowledge of the contact situation point to West Africa as the major sphere of grammatical influence.

3. Valdman (1976:113) cites a song from the Dominican Republic that is not said to be of creole origin; the creole version of the Parable of the Prodigal Son (1976:115); and proclamations made by French authorities (1976:114, 118).

4. I do not mean to suggest that none of the creole speakers were ever exposed to a Portuguese pidgin (cf. Thomason and Kaufman 1975:20n.). On the contrary, the existence of such a pidgin is the most likely explanation for the fact that we find a number of words of Portuguese origin in the Caribbean creoles. However, this influence on the lexical level does not imply that the creoles descended from such a pidgin.

5. 'We are dealing with a French cast in the mold of African syntax, or, as one generally classifies languages according to their syntactic relationships, with an Ewe language with French vocabulary'.

6. Like Hall, Sylvain also believes that the French input into creoles was "simplified" (1936:36).

7. The following abbreviations will be used to identify languages in the citation of examples: H = Haitian Creole; J = Jamaican Creole; E = Ewe; Y = Yoruba; I = Igbo; T = Twi; K = Kpelle; G = Gullah; Ef = Efik; P = Papiamentu. Sources are abbreviated to the right of items in the following manner: (C49) = (Christaller 1875:49); (G28) = (Goilo 1972:28); (H60) = (Hall 1953:60); (H(66)78) = (Hall 1966:78); (V315) = (Valdman 1970:315); (W286) = (Welmers 1973:286).

Many of my questionnaire items were English translations of sentences from Hall (1953) and Valdman (1970), and I had my Haitian informant verify that the Haitian counterparts were genuine examples of current colloquial creole and that the translations were correct. For these examples I have preserved the orthographies of the original sources despite certain differences between them. Occasional secondary source examples for other creoles and West African languages are also written as in the sources from which they were taken. All remaining data are given in the standard orthographies that my informants used.

8. For additional examples, see Baudet 1976 and in preparation.

9. Douglas Taylor (1945) has claimed that the Carib language spoken in the Lesser Antilles had significant morphological influence on Dominican Creole. A thorough search for sources of grammatical structures in the Caribbean creoles should not overlook the possibility of contributions from the Amerinidian languages spoken in the Caribbean at the time of the African arrivals.

REFERENCES

Albó, X. 1970. Social Constraints on Cochabamba Quechua. Cornell University Ph.D. dissertation.

Alleyne, M. C. 1971. Acculturation and the Cultural Matrix of Creolization. In *Pidginization and Creolization of Languages,* D. Hymes, ed., pp. 169-86.

Allsopp, R. 1976. The Case for Afrogenesis. Paper presented at the Conference on New Directions in Creole Studies, University of Guyana.

Andersen, R. W. Forthcoming. Two perspectives on Pidginization as Second-Language Acquisition. In *New Dimensions in Research on the Acquisition and Use of a Second Language,* R. W. Andersen, ed. Rowley, MA: Newbury House Publishers.

Anonymous. 1930. *Glossaire du parler français au Canada.* Québec: Action Sociale.

Bailey, C.-J. 1973. *Variation and Linguistic Theory.* Arlington, VA: Center for Applied Linguistics.

Bailey, C.-J. and K. Maroldt. 1977. The French Lineage of English. In *Langues en contact: pidgins, créoles/languages in contact,* J. M. Meisel, ed., pp. 21-53.

Baudet, M. M. 1976. The Case for an African Substratum in French-Based Caribbean Creoles. University of Pittsburgh M.A. thesis.

———. In preparation. The Grammatical Origins of Martinican Creole. University of Pittsburgh Ph.D. dissertation.

Bernabé, J. 1977. Ecrire le créole. *Môfwaz* 1.11-29.

Bickerton, D. 1974. Creolization, Linguistic Universals, Natural Semantax and the Brain. *Working Papers in Linguistics* 6.124-41.

———. 1975. *Dynamics of a Creole Continuum.* London: Cambridge University Press.

———. 1977. Pidginization and Creolization: Language Acquisition and Language Universals. In *Pidgin and Creole Linguistics,* A. Valdman, ed., pp. 49-69.

Bickerton, D. and C. Odo. 1976-77. *Change and Variation in Hawaiian English,* Vols. 1-2. University of Hawaii: Social Sciences and Linguistic Institute.

Bollée, A. 1977. *Le créole français des Seychelles.* Beihefte ZRP, 159. Tübingen: Max Niemeyer Verlag.

Brueyre, L. 1878. Compère bouc et compère lapin: conte nègre. *Mélusine* 1.495-98.

Brunot, F. and C. Bruneau. 1949. *Précis de grammaire historique de la langue française.* Paris: Masson.

Carcoforo, E. 1935. *Elementi di Somalo e Ki-Suahili parlati al Benadir.* Milano: U. Hoepli.

Cassidy, F. G. 1961. *Jamaica Talk: Three Hundred Years of the English Language in Jamaica.* London: MacMillan.

———. 1971. Tracing the Pidgin Element in Jamaican Creole (with notes on method and the nature of pidgin vocabularies). In *Pidginization and Creolization of Languages,* D. Hymes, ed., pp. 203-21.

Chaudenson, R. 1973. Pour une étude comparée des créoles et parlers français d'outre-mer: survivance et innovation. *Revue de Linguistique Romane* 37. 342-71.

———. 1977. Toward the Reconstruction of the Social Matrix of Creole Language. In *Pidgin and Creole Linguistics,* A. Valdman, ed., pp. 259-76.

Christaller, J. G. 1875. *A Grammar of the Ashante and Fante Languages.* (Reprinted 1964, Ridgewood, NJ: Gregg Press.)

Clapin, S. 1894. *Dictionnaire canadien-français.* (Reprinted 1974, Québec: Laval.)

Conklin, H. C. 1962. Lexicographical Treatment of Folk Taxonomies. In *Problems in Lexicography,* F. W. Householder and S. Saporta, eds. Bloomington, IN: Indiana University Research Center in Anthropology, Folklore, and Linguistics, 21.119-41.

DeCamp, D. 1971. Toward a Generative Analysis of a Post-Creole Continuum. In *Pidginization and Creolization of Languages,* D. Hymes, ed., pp. 349-70.

Diebold, R. A. 1961. Incipient Bilingualism. *Language* 37.97-112.

Dubois, J. and F. Dubois-Charlier. 1970. *Eléments de linguistique française: syntaxe.* Paris: Larousse.

Escure, G. 1978. Vocalic Changes in the Belizean English-Creole Continuum and Markedness Theory. *Berkeley Linguistics Society* 4.283-92.

———. 1979. Linguistic Variation and Ethnic Interaction in Belize: Creole Carib. In *Language and Ethnic Relations,* H. Giles and B. Saint-Jacques, eds. Oxford: Pergamon Press, pp. 107-16.

Ferguson, C. A. 1971. Absence of Copula and the Notion of Simplicity: A Study of Normal Speech, Baby Talk, Foreigner Talk, and Pidgins. In *Pidginization and Creolization of Languages,* D. Hymes, ed., pp. 141-50.

Ferguson, C. A. and C. E. DeBose. 1977. Simplified Registers, Broken Language, and Pidginization. In *Pidgin and Creole Linguistics,* A. Valdman, ed., pp. 99-125.

Forbes, S. 1911. *The Bay Men of Belize and How They Wrested British Honduras from the Spaniards.* London: Society for Promoting Christian Knowledge.

Fortier, A., ed. 1895. *Louisiana Folk-Tales.* Boston: American Folklore Society.

Germain, R. 1976. *Grammaire créole.* Villejuif: Editions du Levain.

Givón, T. 1979. Prolegomena to Any Sane Creology. In *Readings in Creole Studies,* I. F. Hancock, ed. Ghent: Story-Scientia, pp. 3-35.

Goilo, E. R. 1972. *Papiamentu Textbook.* Aruba: Dewit N. V.

Goodman, M. F. 1964. *A Comparative Study of Creole French Dialects.* The Hague: Mouton.

Greenberg, J. H. 1966. *The Languages of Africa.* Bloomington, IN: Indiana University Press.

Gumperz, J. 1977. Sociocultural Knowledge in Conversational Inference. In *Georgetown University 28th Round Table on Languages and Linguistics.* Washington, DC: Georgetown University, pp. 191-212.

Hall, R. A., Jr. 1953. *Haitian Creole: Grammar, Texts, Vocabulary.* Philadelphia: Memoirs of the American Folklore Society, 43.

———. 1966. *Pidgin and Creole Languages.* Ithaca, NY: Cornell University Press.

Hancock, I. F. 1969. A Provisional Comparison of the English-Derived Atlantic Creoles. *Sierra Leone Language Review (African Language Review)* 8.7-72.

———. 1971. A Study of the Sources and Development of the Lexicon of Sierra Leone Creole. University of London: School of Oriental and African Studies Ph.D. dissertation.

Hatch, E. 1978. *Second Language Acquisition: A Book of Readings.* Rowley, MA: Newbury House Publishers.

Hattiger, J. L. 1978. Contribution à l'étude des déterminants du nom en Français populaire d'Abidjan. MS. Abidjan: Institut de Linguistique Appliquée.

Hazaël-Massieux, G. 1978. Approche socio-linguistique de la situation de diglossie français-créole en Guadeloupe. *Langue Française* 37.106-8.

HPD (Heidelberger Forschungsprojekt "Pidgin-Deutsch"). 1978. The Acquisition of German Syntax by Foreign Migrant Workers. In *Linguistic Variation: Models and Methods,* D. Sankoff, ed. New York: Academic Press, pp. 1-22.

Heine, B. 1973. *Pidgin-Sprachen in Bantu-Bereich.* Berlin: D. Reimer Verlag.

Herskovits, M. J. 1958. *The Myth of the Negro Past.* Boston: Beacon Press.

Holm, J. 1978. The Creole English of Nicaragua's Miskito Coast: Its Sociolinguistic History and a Comparative Study of Its Lexicon and Syntax. University of London: University College Ph.D. dissertation.

Hull, A. 1975. On the Origin and Chronology of the French-Based Creoles. Paper presented at the International Conference on Pidgins and Creoles, Honolulu.

Hymes, D., ed. 1971. *Pidginization and Creolization of Languages.* London: Cambridge University Press.

Jackendoff, R. 1975. Morphological and Semantic Regularities in the Lexicon. *Language* 51.639-71.

Jakobson, R. 1963. *Essais de linguistique générale.* Paris: Editions de Minuit.

Kay, P. and G. Sankoff. 1974. A Language-Universals Approach to Pidgins and Creoles. In *Pidgins and Creoles: Current Trends and Prospects,* D. DeCamp and I. F. Hancock, eds. Washington, DC: Georgetown University Press, pp. 61-72.

Kenya Population Census. 1969. 3 Vols. Republic of Kenya: Statistics Division, Ministry of Finance and Economic Planning.

Labatut, R. 1976. *La phrase peule et ses transformations.* University of Paris Ph.D. dissertation.

Labov, W. 1965. On the Mechanism of Linguistic Change. In *A Reader in Histor-*

ical and Comparative Linguistics, A. Keiler, ed. New York: Holt, Rinehart and Winston, pp. 267-88.

———. 1966. *The Social Stratification of English in New York City.* Washington, DC: Center for Applied Linguistics.

———. 1972a. *Sociolinguistic Patterns.* Philadelphia: University of Pennsylvania Press.

———. 1972b. *Language in the Inner City: Studies in the Black English Vernacular.* Philadelphia: University of Pennsylvania Press.

———. 1974. On the Use of the Present To Explain the Past. In *Proceedings of the Eleventh International Congress of Linguists,* L. Heilmann, ed. Bologna: Il Mulino.

Lafage, S. 1976. Le français écrit et parlé en pays ewe (Sud-Togo). University of Nice Ph.D. dissertation.

Lane, G. 1935. Notes on Louisiana French, 2: The Negro-French Dialect. *Language* 11.5-16.

Larocque-Tinker, E. 1956. Le cajun et le gombo. *La Revue de Paris* April 63.92-103.

Lavandera, B. 1974. On Sociolinguistic Research in New World Spanish: A Review Article. *Language in Society* 2.247-337.

LePage, R. B. 1960. An Historical Introduction to Jamaican Creole. *Creole Language Studies* 1.3-124.

———. 1977. Processes of Pidginization and Creolization. In *Pidgin and Creole Linguistics,* A. Valdman, ed., pp. 222-55.

LePage, R. B. and D. DeCamp. 1960. *Jamaican Creole.* Creole Language Studies I. London: MacMillan.

Manessy, G. 1978a. Le français d'Afrique noire, français créole ou créole français? *Langue Française* 37.91-105.

———. 1978b. Observations sur un corpus de français oral recueilli dans le Sud du Cameroun. *Bulletin du Centre d'Etude des Plurilinguismes,* I.D.E.R.I.C., University of Nice, 5.1-32.

Marbot, F. 1869. *Les Bambous: nouvelle édition.* Fort-de-France: Librairie F. Thomas. (Reprinted 1976, Tournai, Belgium: Casterman.)

Martinet, A. 1955. *Economie des changements phonétiques.* Berne: Francke.

———. 1961. *A Functional View of Language.* Oxford: Clarendon Press.

———. 1975. *Evolution des langues et reconstruction.* Paris: Presses Universitaires de France.

Meisel, J. M., ed. 1977. *Langues en contact: pidgins, créoles/languages in contact.* Tübingen: TBL Verlag, G. Narr.

Mercier, A. 1880. Etude sur la langue créole en Louisiane. (Reprinted Comptes rendus, *l'Athénée louisianais,* pp. 378-97.)

Mintz, S. 1971. The Socio-Historical Background to Pidginization and Creolization.

In *Pidginization and Creolization of Languages,* D. Hymes, ed., pp. 81-496.

Morgan, R. 1960. The Lexicon of St. Martin Creole. *Anthropological Linguistics* 2.7-29.

———. 1979. Guadeloupean Creole Pronouns: A Study of Expansion in Morpho-Syntactic Structure. Paper presented at the Conference on Theoretical Orientations in Creole Studies, St. Thomas.

Mühlhäusler, P. 1980. Structural Expansion and the Process of Creolization. In *Theoretical Orientations in Creole Studies,* A. Valdman and A. R. Highfield, eds., pp. 19-55.

Muysken, P. 1977. *Syntactic Developments in the Verb Phrase of Ecuadorian Quechua.* Dordrecht: Foris Publishers.

———. 1979. Substratum and Stratification: The Gerund in Ecuadorian Rural Spanish. Paper presented at the 43rd Conference of the Americanists, Vancouver.

———. Forthcoming. Sources for the Study of Amerindian Contact Languages in Ecuador. *Amsterdam Creole Studies* 3.

Obilade, A. O. 1977. Nigerian Pidgin: A Case of Unusual Depidginization. Paper presented at the Twelfth International Congress of Linguists, Vienna.

Parsons, E. C. 1936. *Folk-lore of the Antilles, French and English.* Vol. 2. New York: American Folklore Society.

Phillips, H. 1978. The Spoken French of Louisiana. In *The Cajuns,* G. R. Conrad, ed. Lafayette, LA: USL, pp. 173-84.

Poirier, P. 1953. *Glossaire acadien, A-B-C.* St. Joseph, NB: University of St. Joseph.

———. 1977. *Glossaire acadien, D-Z.* 4 vols. Moncton: University of Moncton.

Pottier, B. 1970. Le domaine de l'ethno-linguistique. *Langages* 18.3-11.

Poutignat, P. and P. Wald. 1978. MS. Français et sango à Bouar 1. Fonctions marginales du français dans les stratégies interpersonnelles.

Poyen-Bellisle, R. de. 1894. *Les sons et les formes du créole dans les Antilles.* Baltimore: J. Murphy.

Reinecke, J. E. 1971. Some Suggested Fields for Research. In *Pidginization and Creolization of Languages,* D. Hymes, ed., pp. 499-501.

Reinecke, J. E., et al. 1975. *A Bibliography of Pidgin and Creole Languages.* Honolulu: Hawaii University Press.

Renaud, P. 1976. Le français au Cameroun: fonctions (et connotations) d'identité et d'identification ethnique des français régionaux et camerounais. *Bulletin du Centre d'Etude des Plurilinguismes* 3.3-7.

Richardson, I. 1961. Some Observations on the Status of Town Bemba in Northern Rhodesia. *African Language Studies* 2.25-36.

Romaine, S. 1980. The Status of Sociolinguistic Theory: Some Historical Considerations. University of Edinburgh Ph.D. dissertation.

Rossé, R. 1977. Le swahili de Lubumbashi. University of Nice Ph.D. dissertation.

Salcède, G. 1977. De quelques similitudes entre l'anglais et le créole. *Môfwaz* 1.51-57.

Sankoff, G. 1979. The Genesis of a Language. In *The Genesis of Language,* K. Hill, ed. Ann Arbor: Karoma Publishers, pp. 23-47.

———. 1980. Linguistic Variation in Pidgin-Creole Studies. In *Theoretical Orientations in Creole Studies,* A. Valdman and A. R. Highfield, eds., pp. 139-64.

Sankoff, G. and P. Brown. 1976. On the Origins of Syntax in Discourse: A Case Study of Tok Pisin Relatives. *Language* 52.631-66.

Schumann, J. 1978. *The Pidginization Process: A Model for Second Language Acquisition.* Rowley, MA: Newbury House Publishers.

Scotton, C. M. 1976. Strategies of Neutrality. *Language* 52.4.919-41.

Sesep N'Sial, B. 1978. Le métissage linguistique français-lingala. University of Nice Ph.D. dissertation.

Shuy, R. W., Wolfram, W. A., and W. K. Riley. 1967. *A Study of Social Dialects in Detroit.* Final Report, Project 6-1347. Washington, DC: Office of Education.

Stark, L. R. and P. Muysken. 1977. *Diccionario español-quichua, quichua-español.* Quito: Museo del Banco Central.

Strangeways, T. 1822. *Sketch of the Mosquito Shore, Including the Territory of Poyais.* Edinburgh: W. Blackwood.

Sylvain (Comhaire-Sylvain), S. 1936. *La créole haïtien: morphologie et syntaxe.* Wetteren, Belgium: Imprimerie de Meester; Port-au-Prince: by the author.

Taylor, D. 1945. Certain Carib Morphological Influences on Creoles. *International Journal of American Linguistics* 15.140-55.

———. 1951. Structural Outline of Caribbean Creole. *Word* 7.43-59.

———. 1963. The Origin of West Indian Creole Languages: Evidence from Grammatical Categories. *American Anthropologist* 65.800-814.

———. 1971. Grammatical and Lexical Affinities of Creoles. In *Pidginization and Creolization of Languages,* D. Hymes, ed., pp. 293-96.

———. 1977. *Languages of the West Indies.* Baltimore: Johns Hopkins University Press.

Thomason, S. G. and T. Kaufman. 1975. MS. Language Contact, Creolization, and Genetic Linguistics. Revised version of "Toward an Adequate Definition of Creolization." Paper presented at the International Conference on Pidgins and Creoles, Honolulu.

Thompson, R. W. 1961. A Note on Some Possible Affinities Between the Creole Dialects of the Old World and Those of the New. *Creole Language Studies* 2.107-13.

Traugott, E. C. 1976. Natural Semantax: Its Role in the Study of Second Language Acquisition. In *Notions of Simplification, Interlanguages and Pidgins and Their Relations to Second Language Pedagogy,* S. P. Corder and E. Roulet, eds., Actes du 5ème Colloque de Linguistique Appliquée de Neuchâtel. Geneva: Librairie

Droz, pp. 132-62.

———. 1977. Pidginization, Creolization and Language Change. In *Pidgin and Creole Linguistics,* A. Valdman, ed., pp. 70-98.

Trudgill, P. 1974. *The Social Differentiation of English in Norwich.* London: Cambridge University Press.

———. In preparation. *Sociolinguistic Context and Language Change.* Oxford: Blackwell.

Valdman, A. 1970. *Basic Course in Haitian Creole.* Bloomington, IN: Indiana University Press.

———. 1971. The Language Situation in Haiti. In *Pidginization and Creolization of Languages,* D. Hymes, ed., pp. 61-62.

———. 1975. A Pidgin Origin for Creole French? Paper presented at the International Conference on Pidgins and Creoles, Honolulu.

———. 1976a. La complexification dans le système des déterminants des parlers franco-créoles. *Bulletin du Centre d'Etude des Plurilinguismes* 4.11-34.

———. 1976b. Créolisation sans pidgin: le système des déterminants du nom dans les parlers franco-créoles. In *Langues en contact: pidgins, créoles/languages in contact,* J. M. Meisel, ed., pp. 105-36.

———, ed. 1977a. *Pidgin and Creole Linguistics.* Bloomington, IN: Indiana University Press.

———. 1977b. Creolization: Elaboration in the Development of Creole French Dialects. In *Pidgin and Creole Linguistics,* A. Valdman, ed., pp. 155-89.

———. 1978a. La créolisation dans les parlers franco-créoles. *Langue Française* 37.40-59.

———. 1978b. *Le créole: structure, statut et origine.* Paris: Klincksieck.

Valdman, A. and A. R. Highfield, eds. 1980. *Theoretical Orientations in Creole Studies.* New York: Academic Press.

Wald, B. 1973. Variation in the Tense Markers of Mombasa Swahili. Columbia University Ph.D. dissertation.

———. 1976. Comparative Notes on Past Tenses in Kenyan Northeast Bantu Languages. *Studies in African Linguistics.* Supplement 6.267-81.

Welmers, W. E. 1973. *African Language Structures.* Los Angeles: University of California.

Westermann, D. 1942-43. *La langue éwé du Togo: Méthode pratique.* Lome: by the author.

Weinreich, U., Labov, W., and M. I. Herzog. 1968. Empirical Foundations for a Theory of Language Change. In *Directions for Historical Linguistics,* W. P. Lehmann and Y. Malkiel, eds. Austin: University of Texas Press, pp. 95-195.

Whinnom, K. 1971. Linguistic Hybridization and the 'Special Case' of Pidgins and Creoles. In *Pidginization and Creolization of Languages,* D. Hymes, ed., pp. 91-115.

Whiteley, W. H. 1969. *Swahili: The Rise of a National Language.* London: Methuen and Co., Ltd.

Williams, W. 1783. *Mr. Penrose: The Journal of Penrose, Seaman.* D. Dickason, ed. (Reprinted 1969, Bloomington, IN: Indiana University Press.)

Wright, J., ed. 1898-1905. *The English Dialect Dictionary.* London: H. Frowde.